PRAISE FOR

GOD LAUGHS

This book is about much more than a catchy title. It is a revelation on the believer's quest to know God more intimately.

Raymond F. Culpepper, D.D
First Assistant General Overseer, Church of God International
Cleveland, Tennessee

Both Elmer Towns and Charles Billingsley minister here at Thomas Road Baptist Church. They are men of prayer and worship, and they love their Lord God with all their hearts. Their book *God Laughs* will bless the hearts of any who read it, because they have told us many different aspects of God that some of us have never thought of. This book will change your life because it will change your relationship to God.

Jonathan Falwell
Senior Pastor, Thomas Road Baptist Church
Lynchburg, Virginia

I love to write music and hymns because it comes out of my heart, and Charles Billingsley is one of my favorite singers because he sings from his heart. I love Dr. Towns because he teaches from his heart. Now they have put together a book called *God Laughs*, which shows the many aspects of the heart of God. This book will intrigue you . . . inform you . . . but most of all it will inspire you to know and respond to God at a higher level.

Don Marsh
Christian Arranger/Composer and Associate Pr
The Center for Worship and Music, Liberty U1
Lynchburg, Virginia

Elmer Towns and Charles Billingsley have written a brilliant book about understanding the intricacies of our great God. I truly believe that *God Laughs* will surprise you. It will certainly entertain you, but more importantly, it is a book that will move you to know God and worship Him more deeply.

Dr. Tom Mullins

Senior Pastor, Christ Fellowship Church
Palm Beach County, Florida

GOD LAUGHS
& 42 MORE
SURPRISING FACTS
ABOUT GOD
THAT WILL CHANGE YOUR LIFE

ELMER L. TOWNS
& CHARLES BILLINGSLEY

Regal

From Gospel Light
Ventura, California, U.S.A.

Published by Regal
From Gospel Light
Ventura, California, U.S.A.
www.regalbooks.com
Printed in the U.S.A.

Library of Congress Cataloging-in-Publication Data
God laughs : and 42 more surprising facts about God that will change your life /
Charles Billingsley and Elmer Towns.
p. cm.
ISBN 978-0-8307-4659-0 (trade paper)
1. God (Christianity) I. Towns, Elmer L. II. Title.
BT103.B48 2009
231—dc22
2008039434

Rights for publishing this book outside the U.S.A. or in non-English languages are administered by Gospel Light Worldwide, an international not-for-profit ministry. For additional information, please visit www.glww.org, email info@glww.org, or write to Gospel Light Worldwide, 1957 Eastman Avenue, Ventura, CA 93003, U.S.A.

To order copies of this book and other Regal products in bulk quantities, please contact us at 1-800-446-7735.

Contents

Finding the Heart of God

Did you know that God sings? Singing stirs our feelings. Singing the blues make us reflective, and singing "God Bless America" stirs up patriotism in us. Some music moves your feet; other songs make you clap your hands. Does music make you laugh? Did you know that God laughs? Did you know that He smiles? Yes, God does all these things—and more—and when you understand why, you'll understand Him better. In this book, we'll reflect on some of these attributes of God so that we can know more about Him.

As you shop, do you touch various garments? Can you tell something about a garment from just touching it? God has human-like traits (see chapter 37). He touches, and He likes to be touched by His people. Do you know the difference between touching a cotton towel and touching a handful of cotton freshly picked from the bush? Each touch is different and each touch does something different to you . . . touch ice to feel cold . . . touch your shiny smooth new car to feel the pride of ownership . . . touch a woman's face to arouse your emotions. We wouldn't be human if touch didn't stimulate us, and God couldn't relate to us if He couldn't be touched, or touch us. Learn something about God from this marvelous sensation. What do you think God feels when He touches? Read on to find out.

When you smell the aroma of hot donuts, are you tempted to buy some? The smell of sizzling hamburgers on a grill makes you hungry. A nauseating smell protects you from eating rotten meat. God enjoys the aroma of good things (see chapter 12). What do you think smell does to God? Read on to learn what God likes to smell.

The ice cream shop uses a taster spoon to entice you to buy a cone. Have you ever tasted three or four flavors just because you like to taste ice cream? Again, God has human-like traits. He likes to taste. What does God like to taste? You don't know? Then read on. There are a lot of things God does, and the more you know, the better you can respond to Him. God sees . . . God winks . . . God hears and God cries! God waits and God runs! God is jealous, and God gets angry. God smiles, and God frowns.

So, is your curiosity tweaked? Keep reading to find out more about the God you obey and worship. Why? Because the more you reflect on God, the more you'll enjoy your service to Him and the more you'll enjoy worshiping Him. You'll become a fulfilled Christian as you reflect on the heart of God.

Written from our homes at the foot of the Blue Ridge Mountains,

Charles Billingsley and
Elmer Towns

God Has a Heart

*And the L*ORD* smelled a soothing aroma. Then the L*ORD* said in His heart, "I will never again curse the ground for man's sake."*
GENESIS 8:21

*The L*ORD* has sought for Himself a man after His own heart.*
1 SAMUEL 13:14

I (Charles) love to sing. It is probably my favorite way to praise the Lord. Certain songs allow me to really belt out some big notes. Yet, other songs are more intimate and subdued. Either way, it is in singing that I really feel the pleasure of worshiping God. When I have the right attitude combined with the right song, I am able to sing with all my heart to the Lord.

I'm sure you have experienced this same feeling. Whether we are alone in our closet of prayer or standing with thousands in a huge conference somewhere, it is a powerful moment to sing from the bottom of the heart and touch the heart of God with our praise.

Did you know God has a heart?

Not a physical organ like ours, but just as our hearts are filled with love for our mother, a special relative or our first sweetheart, so too God has a heart that reaches out to those He loves. God has a heart that directs all He does. Just as our hearts overflowed with love on the day of our wedding, so God's heart overflows to us on special days such as the day of our conversion.

I'm overwhelmed when I think of the sacrificial love a mother has for her baby. She goes through excruciating pain for her baby, sacrificing her time and sometimes her occupation for her baby. God has this same kind of love for us. Think of the sacrifices He made. Jesus gave up His magnificent home in heaven because of His sacrificial love. He endured pain and suffering on the cross. He even made the ultimate sacrifice—giving His life—so that we might be forgiven. When you remember the sacrifices Jesus has made, you can begin to comprehend His unselfish love. *Lord, I bow to You from a passionate heart.*

I have two children whom I love with all my heart. There's nothing I wouldn't do for them and if you watch us walking through a toy store, you'd think there's nothing I wouldn't buy for them. I want them to have everything they need and want (within boundaries). Then I read that my heavenly Father wants to give *me* everything I need and want (within His will). The Scripture says, "Your Father knows what you have need of before you ask Him" (Matt. 6:8).

Because my heavenly Father loves me wholeheartedly, He's given me the privilege of prayer. He invites me, saying, "Ask, and it will be given to you; seek, and you will find; knock, and it will be opened to you" (Matt. 7:7).

Wholehearted love is wonderful. I sing my wholehearted love to God because He first loved me wholeheartedly. *Lord, I revel in my relationship with You.*

In response, God wants our wholehearted dedication to Him. Just as an Old Testament believer had to sacrifice a whole lamb to God in worship, so too God wants us to sacrifice our whole heart, body and soul to Him. Paul says, "I beg you to sacrifice your whole self to God because He has been so merciful to you" (Rom. 12:1, *AMP*).

Next God wants us to serve Him wholeheartedly with our time, talents and treasures. Paul preached, "And whatever you do, do it heartily, as to the Lord and not to men" (Col. 3:23).

Finally, we must praise and worship God wholeheartedly. When we bow in worship, there must be nothing between our soul and the Savior.

My Time to Pray

Lord, I come into Your presence to worship You wholeheartedly;
I give You everything I have—everything;
I give all my money (treasure) to Your control;
I will spend it only as You direct me.
I give You all of my time;
I will spend my time only as You direct me.
I give You all of my talents to accomplish Your will;
I will use my gifts as You direct me.
Take my praise and be glorified in the worship I bring.
Amen.

God Has a Face

When You said, "Seek My face," my heart said to You, "Your face,
LORD, I will seek." Do not hide Your face from me.
PSALM 27:8-9

Until its collapse in 2003, the "Old Man of the Mountain," a rock formation that jutted out from Cannon Mountain, sat overlooking Profile Lake in New Hampshire. The Native American Indians who originally lived in the valley believed that the stone face was a sign of a man who would come to the valley and bring much good for its inhabitants.

There is a story told about the old stone face. In this story a young boy sat for hours studying every feature of the stone face in the rock. The face in the cliff was the semblance of a person who would come and do great things, and the boy wanted to be the first to recognize the one who would bring good to the valley. The longer the boy memorized the features, the surer he became that he'd be the first to recognize the stone face when he arrived.

One day a peddler came to town selling his wares, including his specialty, a snake oil that promised to heal many diseases. The boy, believing that this was the man the mountain had foretold, went running down the one street of town telling everyone the stone face was coming. The peddler sold many bottles of his "healing oil" that day. However the boy and the town soon realized that the oil didn't hold any miraculous cure, and they became disillusioned.

Years later, another man came through town selling shares to a promised railroad that would bring prosperity to the region. Again, the boy ran up the road yelling that stone face was coming. The man left town with the people's money, but the railroad never came. The boy became disillusioned again. "It's just a myth," he told himself.

Eventually the boy went off to college, and in the early colonial days, only the churches began colleges. There a great revival occurred, and the boy became a Christian. God called the boy into ministry, and so the boy went back to his hometown to tell them the good news of Jesus Christ.

The boy, now grown into a young man, returned to his hometown. He greeted the blacksmith, but the blacksmith didn't return his greetings. He only stared. The same thing happened when he greeted a lady hanging her wash on a line. Repeatedly, people didn't speak, but stared at him, seemingly in disbelief.

At first the young man thought they were against him because he had written to tell his family that he would preach the gospel in his hometown.

But no—the people stared because the young man's face has grown into the likeness of the great stone face. And the boy, now the man in the stone face, had come to bring goodness to the valley; he had come to preach Jesus unto them.

The deeper truth: *We become like the person we spend our life gazing upon.*

God has a face and He has told us to "seek ye My face" (Ps. 27:8, *KJV*).

Because God is holy, when we meditate on Him, we will slowly become holy like God. God has a heart—a good heart—

and the more we contemplate God, the more our heart becomes like His heart. So God wants us to spend time reflecting on Him so we will become like Him.

How do we get a heart like God's? Solomon told us in Proverbs, "As in water, face reflects face" (Prov. 27:19, *NASB*). That means that when you look into water, you see an image of your face looking back at you. But when you look into the face of God, do you see God looking back at you? Then you make corrections in your attitudes or actions according to what you see in God's face, and that process will make you become like God. *O Lord, help me see You so I can become like You.*

There is only one man in Scripture who is recorded as seeing God's face. The Bible recounts, "So the LORD spoke to Moses face to face" (Exod. 33:11). How did that happen? No man had ever done that before.

As Moses was praying, he asked, "Please, show me Your glory" (Exod. 33:18). God answered Moses with what we've all heard in our churches: "You cannot see My face; for no man shall see Me, and live" (v. 20). This is a predicament. How can God say in Psalm 27:8, "Seek My face," while previously saying, "No man shall see Me, and live"?

Let's try to understand this by taking a closer look at what happened to Moses. Because of his integrity and ability to intercede, part of Moses' request was answered. God took Moses to the top of Mount Sinai, put him into a split rock and allowed the glory of God to pass in front of him. Then to save Moses' life, God used His hand to cover Moses. As the glory of God passed away from Moses, God removed His hand and Moses saw the backside of God.

Moses saw what no human had ever seen.

When Moses came down from Mount Sinai, the people were terrified of him. "Now it was so, when Moses came down from Mount Sinai (and the two tablets of the Testimony were in Moses' hand when he came down from the mountain), that Moses did not know that the skin of his face shone while he talked" (Exod. 34:29). Moses had been in the presence of God and seen His glory. He became like the person he passionately desired to gaze upon.

For 40 days, Moses had to put a veil over his face when he talked to people because "they were afraid to come near him" (Exod. 34:30).

For Moses it was a physical experience of being face to face with God. He went to the top of Mount Sinai that was covered with the Shekinah cloud of glory. God was *actually* there. Moses talked with God audibly and directly heard His words.

But we're different. We come to God spiritually. We can't see the physical features of God's face for God is Spirit (see John 4:23), but we can talk to God in prayer. Our inner spirit can feel God's presence, and we can know what He is saying to us.

Plus we have something Moses didn't have: the words of God written in Scripture. When we read the words of God in the Bible, He is speaking to us. When we reflect on the heart of the Lord, we experience His presence in prayer.

There is a thing called the *atmospheric presence of God*. I (Charles) often feel it when leading praise and worship songs. The Bible says, "The Father wants this kind of worship from us" (John 4:24, *TLB*). There was a famous line from the movie *Field of Dreams* that said, "If you build it, they will come." I'd like to paraphrase it into my own expression: "If you worship the Father, He will come to receive it." When the Father comes, I call it *atmospheric worship*.

I (Elmer) have often felt the same presence of God when preaching. During the preaching service, He seems to be walking among the pews. Lives are being touched. Hearts are being changed. It's the atmospheric presence of God. *Lord, as I read the pages of this book, may I feel Your presence and may You transform my life.*

We need to feel God's presence when we worship Him, even in a small way. We know we are sinners, and none of us are perfect. None of us has perfect understanding of all things, but by searching for God's face, we can begin to become more like Him. "For now we see in a mirror, dimly, but then [in heaven] face to face" (1 Cor. 13:12). Only the Lord perfectly knows all things. I want to try to understand Him. I want to please Him.

So my prayer today is, "*Hide Your face from my sins*" (Ps. 51:9), for if He were to judge me for my sin, I could not stand before Him. I need the Lord to forgive all my rebellious sins and my innocent sins.

My next prayer is, "*Do not hide Your face from me*" (Ps. 102:2). I want to experience His atmospheric presence and learn His ways. I need for Him to open my eyes so that I may learn from Scripture.

Then I want to be holy like the Lord. I want to know God and get close to Him. I want to walk with God and enjoy fellowship with Him. When He tells me to seek His face, I will seek His presence.

Finally, my prayer is to have God's full blessing on my life, family and service. "*Make Your face shine upon Your servant*" (Ps. 119:135).

My Time to Pray

Lord, I'm looking forward to seeing something in heaven
I can't see while here on earth.
Lord, I'm looking forward to seeing something
You promised me in Your Word.
Lord, You have promised in Scripture,
"His servants shall worship Him.
They shall see His face . . ." (Rev. 22:3-4, AMP).
Amen.

3

God Sings

For the Lord your God has arrived to live among you. He is a mighty Savior. He will rejoice over you in great gladness; he will love you and not accuse you. Is that a joyous choir I hear? No, it is the Lord himself exulting (rejoicing) over you in happy song.
ZEPHANIAH 3:17, *TLB*

I (Charles) was nervous and was sure I wouldn't be able to sing a note, especially considering the situation. My fiancée, Shae, and I were sitting in the front seat of my dad's new Lexus sedan, overlooking the Salt Lake City valley. It was a perfect setting after having a perfect meal on top of Snowbird Lodge in Little Cottonwood Canyon.

I had planned this event for a long time, and the moment had finally come for me to ask her hand in marriage. I planned to begin by singing a song I had written just for her. But my throat got dry. The doctors say dry throat is caused by nervousness. The more nervous I got, the drier my throat became. I was wishing with all my heart that my mouth were as wet as my armpits! It's funny, I sing almost every day of my life for crowds of every size and I don't get nervous. But on this night . . . I was terrified!

So, I did what every brave and fearless man would do: I turned the tape over and played the demo. I clasped her by both

hands and said, "Can I play you a song I wrote?" So I hit the
button and together we watched the sun set to this song:

"Forever in Love"
Stepped down off the plane from Salt Lake City
What had only been a week felt like eternity
Since I'd seen your smiling face, or felt your warm embrace
Or heard the tender words that said, "You'd missed me."
I looked into your eyes and they were teary
Then it stirred within my soul and I knew that we would be
In this living fairy tale . . . our hearts would never fail
For God had made this love our destiny

So I will stand by your side forever
And I will lift up your life as long as we're together
I will put trust in you and everything you do
Cause I'm forever in love with you

By this time we were both crying and I was beginning to
gain confidence. The song was working! I was watching her
melt before my eyes as the second verse began:

Ten years down the road I plan to be
Settled in with children, living my life long dream
And in every circumstance, whenever I have the chance
I'll spend my moments with you . . . faithfully.

And she said yes! It was a wonderful, tender moment for
us. Six months later, I would sing that same song to her at our
wedding. This time, my throat wasn't dry, but neither were my
eyes. I believed and felt every note. Now as I look back at those
lyrics, I realize I am living every word. Wow! God is good.

I am asked all the time if I sing to my wife. The truth is . . . I don't. She hears me enough at church and in concerts, but when our two boys were little, I would sing to them every night. It seemed to bring them comfort and help them relax. Then I realized the Lord loves to sing over us just as I love to sing over my children.

Can you imagine God singing? Do you think He is a tenor, bass or baritone? What kind of song does He sing? When does He sing? What motivates God to sing? I laugh when I look at these questions. If ever there would be a perfect voice, it would be God's. When I think of all the reasons why I sing, it helps me realize why God sings, and maybe even how God sings.

Sometimes, I sing when I'm happy. Children on the way to camp sing camp songs because they anticipate a week of fun, adventure and getting away from home. They sing with laughter and anticipation. Does God sing with laughter and anticipation over what He's going to do for us?

Some sing because they're in love. Picture a young girl with her first boyfriend. She feels as though she's running through a flowery meadow on a bright sunny day. Her feet barely touch the ground. She's singing on perfect pitch. Her songs represent pure joy, anticipation of marriage and the happiness she will have with the man of her dreams. Do you think that God sings a love song in anticipation of His love-relationship with us?

Then again other people sing because of their sadness, and their music is a wail that expresses the sorrows and trials of life. Think of the old spiritual composed in slavery, "Nobody Knows de Trouble I See." While bound in chains, the slaves sang out of hope for better days to come. They sang about their troubles and the anticipation of meeting their Lord in death. Do you think the Lord sings a sad song because of our bondage to sin and our slavery to Satan?

Other times a song can express a story or drama, such as Broadway musicals or the classic operas. Some sing a song of daily works such as Dolly Parton's "9 to 5," while others sing a song of relaxation and sports like "Macarena" or "Take Me Out to the Ballgame." In each of these songs, we tell what we've been doing or the things we want to do. Do you think God sings over us to carry out His work of salvation in our lives?

Sometimes we sing patriotic songs to stir our devotion to our country or cause. We sing "God Bless America" to invoke the Almighty's blessing on our nation or we "Pledge Our Allegiance" with singing. Sometimes our song declares that we will fight for our country. Patriotic music stirs our allegiance, and it makes our feet want to march. Do you think God sings to get us to pledge our allegiance to the Kingdom of heaven?

There are times when we sing a lullaby to put a baby to sleep. Our singing puts everything out of his infant mind, so he will rest and drift into sleep. We sing softly and melodically to soothe a baby's irritation or crying. Do you think God sings a lullaby over us to soothe away our hurts and fears?

Sometimes we sing because we are full of joy and happiness. At a birthday party, we join in to sing "Happy Birthday." At other times, people sing to communicate a message. Perhaps you remember the hippies of the 1960s who sang anti-war songs because they hated the Vietnam War or more recently the Dixie Chicks who penned their songs against the Iraqi War.

Christians sing evangelistic songs to motivate people to get saved or missionary songs to challenge people to carry out the Great Commission. Do you think God sings because He has a message He wants us to give out?

Notice what the Bible says about God singing: "The Lord himself [is] exulting over you in happy song" (Zeph. 3:17, *TLB*). This verse tells us that God rejoices over us, so God sings because we have done something to make Him rejoice. *Lord, I want to make You happy.*

Have you ever thought that you could make God happy? God rejoices when we keep His commandments wholeheartedly. *Lord, make me obedient.*

Most of the verses in the Bible tell us to rejoice in the Lord, but in a few occasions God rejoices (see Ps. 60:6). The Lord rejoices when we are married to Him in salvation, just as a bride rejoices in her coming marriage (see Isa. 62:5). Also, the Lord gets pleasure out of His creations: "The LORD shall rejoice in His works" (Ps. 104:31, *KJV*).

Deuteronomy 30 tells of the curses God puts upon His people for disobeying Him. But God rejoices if they will "again obey the voice of the LORD and do all His commandments" (Deut. 30:8). God will restore His blessings, their farms will prosper and they will enjoy the fruit of their labor. But most of all, "The LORD will again rejoice over you for good" (Deut. 30:9). God gets happy when His children repent and come back to Him.

When someone praises the Lord, does God rejoice with that person? When they "sing praises to him" (Ps. 149:3), what happens? The Bible says, "For the Lord takes pleasure in His people" (Ps. 149:4). So when people sing and rejoice, God takes pleasure in them, and in return, He sings over them. *Lord, I sing to You, and I want You to sing over me.*

There is a relationship between God's joy and our joy. God gives us His joy when we obey His Word. When that happens, we have the joy of God filling our hearts. Jesus said, "These things have I spoken unto you that my joy might remain in you and that your joy may be full" (John 15:11, *KJV*). *Lord, fill me with Your joy.*

So don't think your happiness originates in you. Don't think, "I'm the one who makes me happy." No, you must remember you're made in the image of God and you get everything from God. Your only real joy or happiness comes from Him. It's only natural for God to be happy, so when you rejoice, you are expressing the joy that the Lord has given to you. So sing joyfully to God. He is singing over you.

My Time to Pray

Lord, it thrills me to know You rejoice over me,
And You rejoice over me in singing.
May I always obey Your commandments
And seek Your presence in worship.
May I give You many reasons to sing over me.
Lord, I know You are the source of rejoicing and happiness.
I live in You because I have Your nature.
I will sing because joy comes from Your presence.
Amen.

4

God Has a Mind

Oh, what a wonderful God we have! How great are His wisdom and knowledge and riches! How impossible it is for us to understand His decisions and His methods! For who among us can know the mind of the Lord? Who knows enough to be His counselor and guide?
ROMANS 11:33-34, *TLB*

I (Elmer) walked away from the nursing home disillusioned. My good friend and colleague didn't recognize me and could not converse with me. I told him a joke we had enjoyed years earlier, and he did not recognize the ironic punch line. He did smile though when I laughed at my own joke.

When someone has Alzheimer's, it's as though they are locked in a dark room where they seem to recognize no one, and we can't break into their darkness to talk to them. Perhaps if something or someone has made an indelible impression on their brain, a little recognition may seep into their consciousness.

Their mind is like an old prison I visited in Dauphin, Manitoba, over 50 years ago. Certain cells that were built on an inner wall didn't get any sunshine all day, but prisoners could look across the hall, out at the window across from them to see sun shining on outside trees. A prisoner who got sun in his window would angle a mirror so that those across the hall could enjoy a little warmth from the sun.

That's what we do when we visit a friend with Alzheimer's; we shine a little sunlight of their past life into their consciousness. And doesn't the warm sun feel good anytime we experience the chill of darkness?

What discouraged me most about my friend was his darkened mind. He had a Ph.D. from Harvard and a law degree from Princeton. He had perhaps the most brilliant mind I had ever encountered. One time in a faculty meeting, a question came up about the meaning of an English word. More than 20 academics couldn't define the word, but my friend not only defined it, he also gave us the root in German and quoted a sentence from the German poet Goethe using the word. Brilliant!

But now, his mind is filled with a barren darkness.

I was despondent, asking, "God, couldn't You have prevented this illness?" I even rationalized, "I'd like to have his mind." I prayed wistfully, "Lord, why couldn't You give me his mind instead of wasting it?"

We must be careful when we ask "Why God?" Only God understands the reasons why He does the things He does. "For who has known the mind of the LORD? Or who has become His counselor?" (Rom. 11:34).

Did you know that God has a mind?

We can lose our memory, but God can't. He will know all things eternally. He will not forget anything.

We can misinterpret facts or hold incorrect opinions, but God can't be wrong. He knows all things perfectly. He even knows all potential outcomes, or those things that might have happened but didn't.

We sometimes have difficulty reasoning out things that later seem so simple. Some things we never reason out, but God's mind is perfect. He always knows the consequences of all actions, and the solution to all problems.

We can corrupt our mind by feeding it false doctrine or propaganda. We can become gullible when we believe the lies people tell us. But God can't believe a lie because God is truth.

The first and greatest power of the mind is to know one's self. At the onset of adolescence, a teenager often asks the question, "Who am I?" But God knows Himself perfectly, so He doesn't have to ask the question.

Besides the question "Who am I?" we face other questions, such as "Why am I here on this earth?" and "Where did I come from?" These are basic questions that every adult needs to answer.

We can't be childish with these questions, like the little boy who ran in the kitchen door to ask his mother, "Where did I come from?" She didn't know how to answer, so she took a moment to decide if her son needed an answer for the creation of Adam or an answer for the birds and bees. Then her son solved her dilemma. "Mikey comes from Milwaukee. I just wanted to know where I came from."

The scientists tell us we use only a small part of our brain. We could all be much smarter if we gave ourselves to investigation, learning, memorization and constant review. We could all solve more problems, answer more questions and provide more help to ourselves and to our fellow man. We could improve our mind with effort, but most of us don't.

There are two problems here. First, we could grow our ability to use our mind, but most of us do not give attention to this area of our life. We offer God a mind that is only half developed or ill-prepared. *Lord, forgive my laziness.*

If God had a carpenter's shop and we were the tools on a workbench, which tool would He pick up and use? If God needed a chisel, He would usually use the sharpest one, as the same would be for a saw, drill or knife. Are you keeping your mind sharp and prepared for God? *Lord, I will sharpen my mind for better use.*

But beyond being sharp, we must also keep our minds clean, just as tools must be cleaned to avoid rust and decay. A carpenter wouldn't reach for a tool dirtied by a spilled drink or garbage on the tool table. No, God would desire a clean tool. *Lord, cleanse my mind and I will be clean.*

But sometimes a man is working upstairs and his wife calls to hang a picture. The tool that he wants is not available; it's down in the basement. So he'll grab the most available tool and will drive a nail with the heel of his shoe. Sometimes God has a job to do, but the Christian Ph.D. is not available and a preacher is not around. God will grab the most available Christian—perhaps uneducated—but available and ready to be used. We never know when, where or how God will use us or need us, so we should always be prepared. *Lord, I'm ready; use me.*

Earlier we said there were two problems. The first was our uneducated mind. Second, we just don't know the Lord. We don't understand His nature or what He wrote. We don't understand His principles of serving others or how we should serve Him. *Lord, I will learn how to serve You.*

Remember, you got your mind from God. We think, reason, remember and learn because we received these abilities from God. While God's mind is perfect, He can't learn. We however must continue to grow in our intellectual abilities.

Some Christians have not grown intellectually nor do they intend to sharpen their mind. They think that yielding to God is enough. God will use us according to our usability. But yielded ignorance is still ignorance. *Lord, I will learn more every day.*

As you reflect on the heart of God, look in the Word of God to see His mind. Learn the power of intelligence and place your mind under the direction of God. *Lord, here are my thoughts; use them for Your glory.*

My Time to Pray

Lord, forgive me for my laziness and pride of ignorance;
Give me a discipline to know You more intimately,
And a passion to be used by You.
Lord, I want to be the best servant I can be.
I will learn as much as I can learn,
And know You as deeply as possible.
Lord, don't let me squander the good mind You've given me,
Or destroy it with sinful things.
Keep my mind sharp for Your service.
Amen.

5

God Is Sometimes Silent

Why do You stand afar off, O Lord?
Why are you silent in times of my trouble?
PSALM 10:1, *AMP*

How long will You forget me, O Lord?
How long will You hide Your face from me?
PSALM 13:1, *AMP*

Jerry Falwell, pastor of Thomas Road Baptist Church for more than 50 years, died suddenly at 10:31 AM on May 15, 2007. As the ambulance rushed to his office, the airwaves at Liberty University were overloaded with activity. It seemed every phone in the university rang at the same time. Everyone quickly heard the news, and everyone's grief was different. Some reacted with explosive weeping; others were too stunned to respond.

Then the announcement went out: students and employees were told to gather in the church sanctuary at 1:30 PM. That's a chapel service everyone would attend. No one would skip this meeting. Jerry was dead, and everyone had questions.

Silently, everyone entered the huge 6,000-seat sanctuary. No one talked; no one whispered. The organ wasn't being played. Those with red eyes caught a glimpse of other eyes still crying, but they cried inwardly. The only sound was rustling of clothes, feet shuffling on the tile and the dull groan of theater seats being occupied. Finally everyone was seated.

Silence.

The only thing we could hear was the sound of silence. When there is no noise, your ears are alert to hearing anything, but there was nothing to hear. Only an occasional cough or sniffle, and then even those coughing tried to muffle their sound.

When silence surrounds you, several different emotions capture your thinking. Usually you focus on why you're being quiet. Everyone was thinking about Jerry. *Why would God take Him? What's going to happen now? Why did this happen?*

Then people's thoughts turned inward. *What will I do? How will this affect my future?*

There was a silence in the room that day even amidst several thousand people. It was not eerie or scary. It was not even threatening. It was simply reverent. Everyone waited in the presence of God, wondering in unison: *God, why did You take Jerry Falwell?*

We all sensed the corporate grief, so the meeting didn't begin immediately. We let silence have its healing ministry.

Why is it that we are told to be silent in God's presence? The Bible says, "The LORD is in His holy temple. Let all the earth keep silence before Him" (Hab. 2:20). Sometimes God doesn't want us to talk to Him or even to praise Him. Sometimes God wants us to be quiet and think about Him. You may think nothing is happening when people are silent, but when the mouth is quiet, the heart, soul and mind can be actively engaged.

In silence, people repent of their sins.

In silence, people meditate on Scriptures and grow spiritually.

In silence, people stand in awe of God.

In silence, people wait for God to speak to them.

Sometimes, God reveals Himself in loud thunder and crashing lightning. In those moments God's loud compelling voice can be heard over the din of daily life. But at other times, God speaks in a still, quiet voice, and it is only in silence that we can hear His message. Doesn't God say, "Be still and know that I am God" (Ps. 46:10)?

There are times when we feel God in His quietness, but we missed Him in the thunderous noise surrounding us. Remember the story of Jesus sending His disciples in a boat into a storm. Because God knows everything—better than a weatherman—Jesus knew a killer storm waited to attack them. When the storm struck, the disciples screamed in panic. I can almost hear them yelling, competing with the sound of the storm. I imagine quite a noise was coming from that little boat.

Then Jesus came walking to them on the water. In the midst of noise, the wind and the crashing waves, Jesus came to them and spoke, "Peace, be still" (Mark 4:39). Can you imagine the emotional shock to the disciples when the stormy lake was instantly transformed into a quiet night? Suddenly the clouds were gone, the moon and stars were twinkling and there was nary a breeze blowing. On a calm lake you can worship and meditate on God. *Lord, calm my storms and give peace to my heart.*

When Jerry Falwell died, everyone focused on his or her hurt and loss. No one realized God was about to do supernatural things for the church. Jonathan—Jerry's youngest son—would immediately step in to carry the church to even greater heights. More than 1,000 people came to receive Christ, and more than 1,200 would join the church in the next five months.

Then there was Jerry Jr., the oldest son who became president and chancellor of Liberty University. The following semester after Jerry Sr. died, attendance reached the first goal that Jerry Sr. had set over 30 years earlier—enrolling 25,000 students at the university. Three months after Jerry Sr. died, over 28,000 students enrolled on campus and in the distance-learning program under Jerry Jr.'s new leadership.

Don't fear silence. It is in the silence that we can hear God speak. Seek silence, for in the quiet place, you'll find God.

"This Quiet Place"
Charles Billingsley

In this quiet place, I'm reminded of the grace
That saved my soul, and made my heart brand new.

And in this quiet hour, I can feel Your holy power
Giving me the strength to know just what to do.

For it's in this quiet place that I've learned to seek Your face,
To deny myself, take up my cross, and follow You.

This quiet place is the closet of my prayers.
Where I can go to God and know
that He is there.
And it's in this quiet place that I find ability to care
For the hurting and the hopeless, present everywhere.

But when I lose compassion that I need
and my fire for souls
Is lost indeed, I go to my knees, to my quiet place and discover
That I have not been there.

My Time to Pray

Lord, thank You for speaking clearly in the Scriptures;
Thank You for silence when I understand Your will.
Lord, thank You for looking beyond my feelings,
To work Your perfect will in my life.
Lord, I wait silently and reverently in Your presence;
Speak, for I am listening for Your voice.
Lord, I will do what You tell me to do.
I want to please You with my life.
Amen.

6

God Thinks
About Us

For I know the thoughts that I think toward you,
says the LORD, thoughts of peace and not of evil,
to give you a future and a hope.
JEREMIAH 29:11

It was nine o'clock at night on a cool June night at Camp Ben Lippen, high in the Smoky Mountains of North Carolina. I (Elmer) had just finished my freshman year at Columbia Bible College and was working to prepare the dining hall for campers the next week.

That night I was washing the winter dust from the dining hall with a bucket, mop and a hose of running water. I was barefooted, wearing only a pair of rolled up blue jeans.

I was a little disgruntled because the other two guys working with me had gone to bed, claiming to be tired. I always liked to complete a job before quitting, so I told them, "You go ahead to the cabin. I'll finish."

Mopping my way across the dining room I came face to face with a tattered blue sign with silver letters. A rusty nail held the sign against a 4 x 4-inch pole:

God
Has a
Plan
for
Your Life.

"Ha," I laughed, and then thought, "Is it God's plan for me to mop the floor while my buddies go to sleep?"

I stood there for a few minutes staring at the sign, thinking about the words. Then I asked myself, "Does God have a plan for my life that includes working while my buddies sleep?"

"Yes," I concluded.

I realized I had to live for God not only in the big things, but in the little things too. Like mopping a floor. I was not responsible for what my buddies did, but I was responsible to God for everything I did.

So, I went back to mopping the floor with new enthusiasm, thinking, "I have to please God in everything, even in mopping the floor."

Do you realize that God thinks about you constantly? He says, "For I know the thoughts that I think toward you" (Jer. 29:11).

Some people don't even realize God thinks. Just as we have the powers of thinking, feeling and choice, God—in whose image we were created—has intellect, emotion and will. When God bent over the lifeless clay man, the one we later called Adam, God breathed Himself into Adam, "and man became a living being" (Gen. 2:7). *Lord, I'm awed at the sight of the divine breathing life into a lifeless clay man.*

God does not have a physical body, but He has the power of mind—He thinks; God has the power of emotions—He loves; God has the power of will—He chooses.

Because God has a mind, He remembers. Because God sees our sins, we pray, "Do not remember the sins of my youth" (Ps.

25:7). You must constantly pray, "Remember me, O Lord" (Ps. 106:4). Isn't that what the thief on the cross asked of Jesus, "Remember me when You come into Your kingdom"?

When we remember, we give effort to recall what we previously experienced. Like the little boy studying for an exam, we memorize so we can recall facts for a test. But God doesn't have to give effort to recall, for if He did, that would say God at one time didn't know everything. That can't happen, for God knows all things without effort. He knows all things at all times.

What else does God do with His mind? He reasons. Didn't He say, "Come now, and let us reason together . . . though your sins are like scarlet, they shall be as white as snow; though they are red like crimson, they shall be as wool" (Isa. 1:18)? When God invites you to reason with Him, He wants you to know what He knows about your sin. When you confess your sins and correct your evil ways by repenting, God knows. When you ask for forgiveness, God cleanses you as white as snow. *Lord, I accept Your invitation.*

Since we are made in the image of God (see Gen. 1:26-27), our ability to think, feel and choose is from God as well. When you look into the mirror each morning to comb your hair, you see an image of yourself. What you see is exactly like you, but it's not you. It's your image. When God looks into your face, He sees His image. In one sense, God sees Himself in us. We're like Him, but we're not God.

God has given us many powers of the mind. You think because God thinks, and your thoughts guide your life. You remember because God knows everything actual and potential. So you bring past experiences into your mind to help you guide today's activities. You have the power of choice because God wills, and as you better understand your choices, you better control your life.

God thinks about you constantly. You are never out of His mind. Though there are billions of people in the world, He can think about everyone at the same time. God is unlimited. No one is ever out of His thoughts. *God, You are overwhelming. You are much bigger than any conception I had of You.*

My Time to Pray

Lord, You have thought up a good plan for my life;
Thank You for thinking good things for me.
I want to know Your plan for my life,
I want the good things You have been thinking.
Lord, teach me to think my thoughts after You,
I yield my thoughts to Your superior plan;
I want to do Your will.
Amen.

7

God Has Unique Plans for Every Unsaved Person

For I know the plans and thoughts I have for you, says the Lord, plans of peace and not evil, to give you a good end.
JEREMIAH 29:11, *AMP*

You will show me the path of life; in Your presence is fullness of joy; at Your right hand are pleasures forevermore.
PSALM 16:11

I (Elmer) was preaching in South Korea at the Bible Baptist Church in Seoul. The pastor, Daniel Kim, took me to play golf at a prestigious club high in the mountains. While on the practice tee I went back to the car for a jacket. It was then I looked in the large caddie room and saw about 50 young ladies "waiting for a bag," a phrase meaning they were waiting for an assignment.

The girl caddies in Korea all wear the same uniform, a pleated skirt and bobby socks with black and white oxfords. In this club, they wore red blazers.

I was assigned a caddie that was stronger than the others because my "American" bag was heavier, and she was the only one fluent in English. As we walked down the first fairway, I asked her name, and then asked if she knew Christ as her Savior.

"Oh yes!" she replied and gave a spontaneous testimony of the impact a gospel tract had on her faith while a student at Korean National University. She began to explain in detail the tract *Four Spiritual Laws* written by Bill Bright. She recited the first law: "God loves you and has a wonderful plan for your life." She had been gripped by the statement, explaining, "Buddha doesn't love me personally and individually." She experienced the love of Christ as she read the tract.

Then she described, "Buddha doesn't have a wonderful plan for my life. I never read anything so compelling in all my life." She had been raised a Buddhist, yet she had never felt a relationship to him, nor did she worship him. The caddie bubbled on with her testimony of joining the Campus Crusade group at her university and witnessing for Christ among unsaved students.

"What's your greatest passion in life?" I asked.

"To meet Bill Bright, shake his hand and tell him how much I appreciate his booklet because I came to know Christ as I read his tract."

"I'll tell him next week," I casually replied. "I have lunch plans with him."

She dropped the golf bag and stood transfixed. "YOU KNOW BILL BRIGHT?" she shouted.

She began to shake and weep, not so much for her love of Bill Bright, but because of her love for Jesus Christ. We stopped right there in the fairway, and she didn't get her composure back until we had prayed. The young girl planned to become a full-time worker with Campus Crusade.

Did you know God has plans for every individual, both believers and unbelievers? That means God has a wonderful plan for your life. Have you found it? Are you following it?

We spend lots of time planning. We plan for vacations and for special nights out with our spouse. We make plans for the direction of our career and the growth of a family business. We like to make a plan for our day, our year, even our lifetime. What are your plans?

But more important than our plans for our day, week or year, God has a plan for our eternity. We need to seek God's plan for our lives. *Lord, I long to know Your will for my life.*

So what can we learn about God's plans for us?

First, God has plans for every person to become a Christian. "[He is] not willing that any should perish" (2 Pet. 3:9). But there is a small problem—we are sinners and sin keeps us from God. The Bible says, "All have sinned" (Rom. 3:23) and Psalm 51 tells us that all people were born sinners: "in sin my mother conceived me" (Ps. 51:5).

But God planned to overcome this sin obstacle. The heavenly Father sent His sinless Son to live among sinful people. It was God's plan for all to be saved: "Behold! The Lamb of God who takes away the sin of the world" (John 1:29).

God has eternal plans for you. Jesus said, "My Father, who has given *them* to Me, is greater than all; and no one is able to snatch *them* out of My Father's hand" (John 10:29). *Lord, I rest in Your plans for my eternal security.*

God has plans of good for His followers. Don't the children pray, "God is great, God is good"? Jesus said, "I have come that they may have life, and that they may have it more abundantly" (John 10:10). The first promise in that verse is "eternal life" in heaven. The second promise is an abundantly good life on earth after we are saved. *Lord, give me abundance in my life as I live for You.*

God lets you choose to follow His plan for your life. Jesus said, "I am the door of salvation, by me you shall enter and be saved, and go in and out (in freedom) to find food to eat" (John 10:9, *AMP*). God doesn't demand that we follow Him, but when we do, our faithfulness is rewarded. *Lord, I need Your deliverance from sin to be free to accomplish good plans for my life.*

God has plans of success for you. Don't we all have dreams for success? A high school girl wants to be homecoming queen, and the high school boy wants to be quarterback on a winning team. And doesn't every insurance sales representative want to be a member of the million-dollar round table? God plans for your success. He promises, "This Book of the Law shall not leave you . . . if you meditate in it day and night . . . then it will make you successful and you will prosper" (Josh. 1:8, *AMP*). *Lord, I will reflect on Your instructions so I can be successful.*

Yes, God has a wonderful plan for every saved and unsaved person. God wants everyone to experience His love and salvation, and become a dedicated disciple of Jesus Christ.

But what happens when we ignore God and stray from His plan? Those who have turned their back on God have missed the wonderful opportunities God wants to provide for them. These people are not doing and being all that God intended for their lives and are perhaps missing out on the impact God intended for them to have on the world.

Just imagine—what if there was no Winston Churchill to rally the Allies against Hitler? What if there was no George Washington to get America through Valley Forge and ultimately win the American Revolution. What if there was no Martin Luther or John Wesley?

Let's think about your life. God loves you and has a special plan for your life that is wonderful. Do you know what it is? God's plan ought to become clearer to you each day of your life. "But the path of the uncompromising believer is like the light of dawn, that shines brighter and clearer until it reaches its full strength of high noon" (Prov. 4:18, *AMP*). As you follow the Lord, His plan for your life will get brighter and brighter.

If you're not aware that God has a plan for your life, then start a twofold process. First, the Bible says you can find God's will and know it: "Understand what the will of the Lord is" (Eph. 5:17). Second, yield your life right now to God. From now on make sure that what you do is what God wants you to do. *Lord, I want to follow Your plan for my life. Show it to me and I will do it.*

God wants you to plan your life in accordance with His plans. Just as an architect draws a blueprint of what he wants to accomplish, so too the workman must slowly construct a building in accordance with the pre-drawn plans. Therefore, you must work diligently to build your life in accordance with God's pre-determined plans. *Lord, I'll study Your blueprint for my life. Then I'll daily build what You pre-determine for me.*

Sometimes a worker runs into problems as he constructs a building. There may be unseen bedrock or an unexpected stream of underground water. When digging a foundation for a dormitory at Liberty University in 2006, such a spring was discovered and the whole dorm was moved hundreds of yards.

In our lives the onset of problems or sin may mean a change of plans. A young man graduated from Liberty University and planned to go to the mission field, but his wife refused. As she was working to put her husband through seminary, she discovered a world of entertainment and fun that she enjoyed. She divorced the future missionary, and he had to change his plans. What happens when sin, or your disobedience, or your laziness, disrupts your plans? *Lord, forgive me when I've messed up. I want to get back into the center of Your plans.*

I (Charles) have a global positioning system (GPS) that gives me directions to any place in America. I love the system because I can find my way to any church, hotel or restaurant with the touch of a button. When I choose a destination, it guides me there on the closest route. But when I miss a turn, a voice says, "Reprogramming." Then it gives me another route based on my new location.

God's plan is much like my GPS. When I take a wrong turn, God doesn't drop me like a hot fajita. No, God wants me to glorify Him and serve Him. He reprograms and gives me the best plan for the rest of my life from my new location. *Lord, thank You for forgiving my past sins and failures. Thank You for every time You've reprogrammed Your plan for my life.*

My Time to Pray

Lord, thank You for the good plans You have for me,
Forgive me when I've sinned and missed Your good things.
I want to turn away from selfishness and evil,
And look to You to guide me by Your plans;
I will follow Your plans as You show them to me.
Lord, thank You for giving me direction and purpose in life
When I was lost and doing my own thing.
Thank You for saving me and giving me a new purpose
To glorify You and serve You in all I do.
Lord, You had a wonderful plan for my life when You saved me.
Help me learn Your plan and do it.
Lord, I find happiness and pleasure in fulfilling Your plan.
Keep me in the center of Your will.
If I ever stray from doing Your plan,
Bring me back and reprogram my life.
Amen.

8

God Remembers
No Longer

I will forgive their iniquity, and their sin I will remember no more.
JEREMIAH 31:34

Young Johnnie got a new slingshot and tried it out in the backyard of his grandmother's farm. He shot at the barn door and missed. He shot at the gate and missed. He shot at some birds flying overhead and missed. Then, he went down by the stream and shot at a snake and missed.

Walking back into the farmyard, he shot at Grandmother's duck and hit it in the head, killing it instantly. He looked both ways and thought, *No one saw me.* He quickly got a shovel out of the tool shed and buried the duck behind the barn.

That night after supper Grandmother asked Johnnie's sister, "Mary Jane, will you wash the dishes?"

"No," she said deviously, "Johnnie likes to wash dishes." Then she whispered to him, "Remember the duck."

Johnnie gladly washed dishes, since he was afraid of what would happen if Grandmother found out that he had killed her pet duck.

The next morning after breakfast, Grandmother asked Mary Jane to sweep the hall and porch. She answered, "No, ma'am, Johnnie likes to sweep." Then she whispered, "Remember the duck."

That week Johnnie swept every morning, washed dishes after every meal and did every other task his sister Mary Jane wanted him to do.

The next Saturday morning, Johnnie couldn't take it any longer. He told his grandmother the story of killing her favorite duck. Through his tears Johnnie sobbed, "I'm sorry."

"I know," Grandmother said, "I was washing dishes at the window when I saw you hit my duck. I saw the panic on your face, and I know you didn't mean to do it."

"Did you give him a nice burial?" Grandmother asked.

"Yes," Johnnie answered, "but why did you wait so long to forgive me?"

"I forgave you the moment I saw the anguish in your face," Grandmother replied, "but I wondered how long you'd stay in bondage to Mary Jane."

Many are in bondage to a sin they committed in the past. They go through life blaming themselves for something they did. Their conscience—their own Mary Jane—whispers, "Remember the duck."

When people are convicted by a past sin, they often spend their life in miserable bondage. Everyone needs to remember the promise of 1 John 1:7: "The blood of Jesus Christ, God's Son, cleanses from all sin." Just as Grandmother forgave Johnnie the moment he killed her duck, so too God forgives us the moment we sin. That's the nature of God's forgiveness.

Instead of enjoying freedom in Christ, some Christians walk around dejectedly in bondage. They are slaves to the sin they have committed.

The Bible says, "I will forgive their iniquity, and their sin I will remember no more" (Jer. 31:34). Notice, it doesn't say God forgets sin. Why? God knows all things at all times. If He forgets and doesn't know, that would breach His nature. If God forgets, He wouldn't be God.

But God can "remember no more." When He does that—He chooses to remember no more—God is still omniscient. He is in charge. Our sins are buried in the deepest sea (see Mic. 7:19). God knows they are there, but He chooses not to remember.

There are two steps to forgiveness. The first is a picture of Grandmother looking out the window to see her favorite duck killed. That's a picture of God looking out the window of heaven to see our sin. He forgives us the moment we sin because "the blood of Jesus Christ, His Son, cleanses us the moment we sin" (1 John 1:7, *AMP*).

The second step is Johnnie going to Grandmother to confess his sin because he has offended her and hurt her. He killed her favorite duck. That's a picture of our going sorrowfully to God to make things right with Him. "If we confess our sins, He is faithful and just to forgive us our sins and cleanse us from all unrighteousness" (1 John 1:9).

God has forgiven us before we confess, but we must come to Him to tell Him we're sorry. We don't confess for God's sake; we confess for our sake.

There's a difference between our *relationship* and our *fellowship* with God. God instantly forgives us when we sin because of our *relationship* to Him. He is our heavenly Father, and we are His children. That can't be broken.

But *fellowship* is another matter. That describes our joyful approach to Him. Nothing can affect our eternal relationship with the heavenly Father, but our sin can convict us and steal our happiness. We must go to Him when our fellowship is broken to tell Him we're sorry and ask God to restore our fellowship.

My Time to Pray

Lord, thank You for the blood of Christ, my Savior
That cleanses me of all sin;
I accept Your grace and walk in mercy;
Thank You for forgiving me before I ask.
But, Lord, when I slip and fall into sin,
I'm sorry for my sin, that I didn't mean to do;
Forgive me and restore my fellowship with You.
Amen.

9

God Reads and Writes

*And I saw God sitting on the Great White Judgment Throne . . .
and the dead stood before God to be judged. The books of works were
opened and the dead were sentenced according to their works.
Then the Lamb's Book of Life was opened and anyone whose
name was not there was cast into the Lake of Fire.*
REVELATION 20:11-15, *AMP*

I (Charles) was recently on a plane from Atlanta to San Diego. It was like any other trip. I lugged my belongings onto the jet, stuffed my bags into the overhead bins and took my seat. I was seated next to a man who greeted me with a half smile and a hello. Then he didn't speak to me for the next four hours. He read his book while I read my usual materials—a Bible and a newspaper.

We began our final approach into San Diego when suddenly the man looked at me and said, "Hi, Charles. I'm Ted Baxter. I have been listening to your music for years and thought I could take these last few hours to observe what you read and how you treat people."

Thankfully, I was innocent and kind that day! It was a serious reminder to me that people are watching our testimony and want us to be authentic Christians.

Did you know God has a record of all your works? Does that mean God writes because there is a record of all we do?

Does it also mean that God can read?

In times past, people wrote by hand. Does that mean God wrote our records by hand? Is God up to date? Do you think God now keeps His records on a computer? Maybe a laptop? That would mean God has learned to type. By the time we update our thinking about God's record, maybe He will keep them on a Blackberry, an iPod or maybe on a device that's not yet invented.

Of course God is not limited by time. Jesus is yesterday, today and forever. Maybe God used an upgraded computer before computers were invented. Just as a computer has files and pages, a voice-activated computer of the future could have written God's records.

Have you ever thought that God doesn't need to write things down? He knows all things perfectly from the beginning. He knows without effort. As a matter of fact, if God had to write things down to remember them, that means at a past time God didn't know everything, because He had to give effort to know them. That meant God was not God-like.

God doesn't write things for His benefit. He keeps records for our benefit. God writes things down and reveals them to us for *our* sake.

When God judges the unsaved, they can never say He is biased, because their record speaks for itself. The unsaved can never say God makes mistakes, because the record is accurate. The unsaved can never say someone changed his or her record; the record is complete and true. And finally, the unsaved cannot say, "I didn't know what I was doing." God's record includes both motives and actions. The Bible says, "They are without excuse" (Rom. 1:20). *Lord, I know my name is written in the Lamb's Book of Life.*

Don't forget that God keeps records to reward His children too. God has a crown of rejoicing for those who win the lost to salvation (see 1 Thess. 1:19-20; Phil. 4:1). Those who bravely endure persecution for Jesus' sake will receive a crown of life (see Rev. 2:10). Those who practice self-discipline will receive an incorruptible crown (see 1 Cor. 9:25). Those who teach and shepherd others will receive the crown of glory (see 1 Pet. 5:1-4), and finally, there is a crown of righteousness for those who love His appearing (see 2 Tim. 4:8). *Lord, it's not a crown I seek; I just want to be with You in heaven.*

Lest you think receiving crowns will be like a military service where men and women are given ribbons to wear proudly, it is not. When we appear before God's throne, we will see that we are not responsible for everything we did that deserves merit. No! God did it through us. Christ deserves our rewards. We will see our unworthiness when we look on the face of Jesus, and the Bible describes that we will "cast [our] crowns before the throne" (Rev. 4:10). *Lord, I give all my rewards to You.*

God sees all we do and writes a record in His book. Then when we appear before His throne, God will have something good to say about every one of His children. No matter how little a person has done, God will have a reward for him. God knows because He cares about every one of us. The Bible promises, "Then each man's praises will come from God" (1 Cor. 4:5).

My Time to Pray

Lord, I know You've forgiven all my sin, because You said,
"The blood of Jesus Christ His Son
cleanses from all sin" (1 John 1:7).
So I will not appear at the Great White Judgment Throne.
Only the unsaved will be judged out of Your books.
Lord, I don't want a prize or reward for serving You
Because Jesus has done so much for me;
It is the least I could do to serve You.
Amen.

10

God Has Unknowable Secrets

And Abraham planted a grove of trees on the edge of the desert at the seven springs of Beersheba (the wells where an oath was promised), and Abraham called on the name of El Olam (the eternal hidden God).
GENESIS 21:33, *AMP*

My (Elmer's) wife, Ruth, was 31 years old when she found out the secret of all secrets about her life. She found out she was adopted. Discovering that secret of her birth was so transforming that it shook her inwardly. She was not the physical child of Elvira and Elton Forbes; they adopted her when she was two months old. Finding out that she was not her mother's daughter finally explained some of the many differences between her and her adoptive parents.

Finding out a secret releases some powerful forces. Ruth had to ask "Who am I?" and she was freed from the biological necessities of her adoptive parents. Since she didn't know—and since has not found out—who her parents were, she was free to become who she wanted to be.

Did you know that God has secrets?

God was first called *El Olam* at the Oasis at Beersheba. The name *Olam* meant God was eternal or "from everlasting to everlasting, you are God" (Ps. 90:2). But *Olam* has a second deeper meaning: "the things forever kept secret." It carries the meaning "God hides" or "The God of eternity can't be understood by humans." It's not that God tries to hide from us, but that we as humans just can't understand all that God is like. Therefore, there is part of God that we can never understand.

We can only know the things of God that He reveals to us, and He doesn't choose to reveal everything about Himself to us all at once.

Ruth's parents didn't tell her she was adopted because there was a pervasive belief that "the baby won't understand" or "the baby won't love you if she finds out she's adopted."

But that's not what Ruth thought. She loved her parents more because they picked her and voluntarily sacrificed for her. Ruth felt special because she was chosen, whereas birth parents don't have a choice with the child they receive.

In Genesis 21, Abraham first called God *El Olam*. In the story, Abraham and his family had travelled to a place called Gerar, where a man named Abimelech was king. The king wanted to make a treaty with Abraham, so he asked Abraham to swear before God that he would not deal falsely with him or any of his descendants. Abraham agreed, but he went on to complain to Abimelech that some of the shepherds who had worked for him had dug some wells at Beersheba in the flat sandy desert of south Israel, and Abimelech's shepherds had violently taken them away. This was perhaps done because the Philistines thought the south desert belonged to them. They treated Abraham as a trespasser (see Gen. 21:22-26). Before they agreed, Abraham brought out seven lambs as a gift to Abimelech, apparently to "buy" the wells so he could live there. "Thus they made a covenant at Beersheba" (Gen. 21:32).

After Abimelech left, Abraham worshiped the Lord, *El Olam*. There were probably a lot of things Abraham didn't understand about God. Perhaps he didn't understand how God would eventually give him the entire Promised Land. Perhaps he didn't understand how the fear of God gripped Abimelech's heart. Could this well be God's down payment to Abraham for the Promised Land, as though God was saying, "I'm giving you the title deed to the well of Beersheba as proof that I will later give you the entire Promised Land"?

This book is about finding and encountering the heart of God. But this chapter is about the things that God won't reveal, and you can't know. There are some secrets God doesn't tell us about. If He did, it might overwhelm us, scare us or paralyze us.

Suppose you knew whom you should marry from infancy. Suppose you knew the day you will die. If these things weren't kept secret, we would miss out on the experiences and growth that will make us into the people God wants us to be. We would never grow to become what God wants us to be, if there were no mystery, no challenge and no threats.

When God does reveal Himself to us, it has a purpose. God has said, "The secret things belong to the Lord our God, but those things which are revealed belong to us and to our children forever, that we may do all the words of this law" (Deut. 29:29). Did you notice why God shows us certain things? It's so we may benefit from them or obey them. *Lord, help me to respond correctly to everything You reveal to me.*

You must worship *El Olam* for who He is and for what He does. *El Olam* may not do things the way we do them, and we can't always understand Him. "For My thoughts are not your thoughts, nor are your ways My ways," says the Lord. When we don't understand, it is important to remember that where our vision is limited and small, God's vision is perfect and eternal. God views the big picture; God sees the grand plan. "For as the heavens are higher than the earth, so are My ways higher than your ways, and My thoughts than your thoughts" (Isa. 55: 8, 9). *Lord, I surrender to Your thoughts and to Your way of doing things.*

But we can learn a wise lesson from Abraham: when Abraham couldn't understand what God was doing in his life, he stopped to worship *El Olam*.

My Time to Pray

Lord, I pause to worship You for Your work
Today in my life and family.
I don't always understand what You are doing
And at times I resist Your plans and purposes.
Lord, forgive me for my selfish struggles against You,
Teach me to trust You when I can't see
What You are doing in my life.
I want You to lead me and give me
The best You want me to have.
Amen.

11

God Whispers

"Go out and stand before me on the mountain," the Lord told him. And as Elijah stood there, the Lord passed by, and a mighty windstorm hit the mountain. It was such a terrible blast that the rocks were torn loose, but the Lord was not in the wind. After the wind there was an earthquake, but the Lord was not in the earthquake. And after the earthquake there was a fire, but the Lord was not in the fire. And after the fire there was the sound of a gentle whisper.
1 KINGS 19:11-12, *NLT*

I (Elmer) married a gentle woman. My wife, Ruth, has never raised her voice or yelled at me. For the longest time, I didn't realize how fortunate I was until I became a pastor and got involved in counseling married couples through their knockdown, drawn out fights. I saw women lose their temper—and their feminine softness—as they yelled at a husband and poured out their "hurt" in moments of uncontrollable rage.

I soon realized how blessed I was. She didn't yell for the kids when she wanted them to come, nor did she raise her voice at them in anger or frustration. She also didn't yell at me, though sometimes she'd quietly write me notes to tell me how she felt. She didn't tell me I was wrong, for that was not her style, but she wanted me to know how she felt about things.

So how did she make the kids do right? She didn't have to yell because the kids knew what she wanted them to do. They could see it in her face or feel it in the atmosphere. Maybe it was the Holy Spirit speaking to them. The kids always knew their mother didn't yell, but they all said, "Watch out when she whispers!"

When people yell at each other, two things happen. First, both turn up the volume to out-yell the other. And second, the more they yell, the less they listen. Don't you think God knows that?

So God seldom yells to get our attention. If God yelled at people, instead of listening, they'd yell right back.

God knows people stop listening to those who yell at them. So when God wants us to listen to Him, what does He do?

God whispers.

Look at the verse at the beginning of this chapter. God came to Elijah with a still, small voice. A whisper is the opposite of loud, bold Elijah. How loud was Elijah? He gathered almost 1,000 prophets of Baal on Mount Carmel for a religious shout-out. Can you hear him yelling a challenge to 950 ungodly prophets? "THE GOD WHO ANSWERS BY FIRE, HE IS GOD" (1 Kings 18:24).

They had a contest to see who could bring fire from heaven. The prophets of Baal went first. They placed their sacrifice on the altar and cried aloud, "O BAAL, HEAR US!" (1 Kings 18:26). But Baal didn't exist—except in name—so he didn't answer.

Sarcastically Elijah prodded them, "Cry aloud . . . either he is meditating, or he is busy . . . or perhaps he is sleeping and must be awakened" (1 Kings 18:27). But yelling didn't get an answer.

Then Elijah prayed, and God answered from heaven with fire. Elijah commanded the crowd, "Seize the prophets of Baal! Do not let one of them escape!" (1 Kings 18:40). The false prophets were executed. In revenge, Queen Jezebel swore she'd have Elijah's head. The bold prophet Elijah ran across the nation Israel, then across Judah, and into the desert where he prayed to die. The spectacular events on Mount Carmel weren't enough to convince Elijah to continue his ministry.

Elijah continued running away. He left the Holy Land and crossed the desert, traveling all the way to the Sinai Peninsula. Was Elijah running from Jezebel? Was Elijah running from his perceived inadequacies? Was Elijah running from God?

Maybe Elijah was running from the call upon his life. When he got to Mount Sinai, he complained to God that he was a failure, saying, "I alone am left; and they seek to take my life" (1 Kings 19:10).

Notice, God didn't run after Elijah, nor did He yell to get his attention. God let Elijah feel the loneliness of his failure. When Elijah was left alone, frustrated and at the end of his rope, then he was ready to listen to God.

God came to Him, but not in a mighty hurricane . . . not in an earthquake . . . and not in a consuming fire. God didn't need noise or force; He already had Elijah's attention. So God whispered.

Why does God whisper? God whispers because He wants our attention. No one likes to be yelled at and we often reject anyone who yells at us or we end up yelling back. *Lord, You have my attention. I'll listen to You.*

Why does God whisper? Because those who yell blur their words and phrases. We hear noise, but we miss the message. God doesn't want us to miss His message, so He whispers. *Lord, I don't want to miss Your message.*

Why does God whisper? Because we get quiet when someone whispers to us. We usually stop what we're doing and focus all our physical attention on the whisperer so we can hear what he is saying. Isn't that why God whispers? He wants us to stop doing what we are doing—whether we're sinning or going about our business—He whispers so we'll stop and focus on Him. *Lord, help me be still so I can listen.*

Why does God whisper? To get us to listen attentively to Him. When He whispers, we focus on His message, more than the words of the message. *Lord, when You whisper, I make You the focus of my life and service.*

My Time to Pray

Lord, You whispered to get Elijah's attention,
And You speak to me quietly in the blackness of night.
I want to hear and know what You say.
Lord, You speak quietly in my heart so I won't miss Your message;
Help me understand what You want me to do.
I will obey Your words and do what You tell me.
I will be your servant.
Amen.

12

God Has a Nose

And the LORD was pleased with the aroma of the sacrifice and said to himself, "I will never again curse the ground because of the human race, even though everything they think or imagine is bent toward evil from childhood. I will never again destroy all living things."
GENESIS 8:21, NLT

What's the sweetest smell in the world? To some women it may be perfume. To some men it may be the grease from a motor they are tuning up. To a mother it might be talcum powder on her baby. What's the sweetest smelling aroma you've ever smelled? A barbeque steak? Hot donuts? An incense candle?

To me (Elmer) one of the best smells ever was breakfast by a Northern Canadian lake. I was president of Winnipeg Bible College and two friends took me fishing in the summer of 1964.

We drove north 100 miles on a paved road, and then I felt the gears shift down as we ran out of pavement and traveled another 50 miles on a sandy road. Then we took off cross-country on a deer trail to an Indian village. There I met our guide, an 81-year-old Indian whose grandfather had been chief of his tribe. My elderly guide asked me, "Would you like to meet my father?"

I was already surprised at the guide's age, so I was intrigued to meet his dad. He took me to meet a 101-year-old man, bent with age and with shriveled skin from too many cold winters. The 101-year-old man advised me, "Eat what my son cooks; you can live as long as I have."

We left the Indian reservation and didn't arrive at an abandoned gold mine until after dark. As you can imagine, there were no convenience stores or snack shops in the Canadian north woods, so although we were hungry, we crawled in our sleeping bags without eating and went immediately to sleep. We were too tired to cook a meal.

I felt my sleeping bag shake the next morning. Quietly, the 81-year-old Indian nodded for me to get up and follow him to a bank overlooking the lake. There was a tiny fire, so small that the solitary flame looked too small to cook anything. Three burning sticks produced a small shaft of smoke curling straight up through the pine trees, since there wasn't a trace of breeze anywhere. An old-fashioned galvanized coffee pot sat in the middle of the three sticks.

Without saying a word the Indian poured me a cup of bubbling hot coffee. I smelled the coffee before trying to sip it.

The smell was so delicious my eyes watered. It was too hot to drink but the aroma was irresistible. I blew and sipped. Still too hot.

So I sat down to embrace the smell.

I've enjoyed a lot of other delectable smells, but that early morning, my guide and the remote setting miles from civilization enhanced my favorite smell.

What about God? What was the most irresistible smell to ever enter the nostrils of God? Maybe the extremity of Noah's sacrifice and the setting made the smell of roasting meat irresistible to God. Noah had lived in the Ark for over a year. Not once did Noah have a chance of offering a burnt sacrifice to God in a boat. We don't know if they had fire for cooking on the ark, or if a burnt sacrifice might have caught the ark on fire.

The first thing Noah did when he planted his sea legs on *terra firma* was to seek fellowship with God.

Noah and his sons gathered stones, and then killed the animals before laying them on the wood on the altar. It was probably a huge pile of brushwood on top of logs. The fire was kindled and the animals were sacrificed to God.

God was pleased when he saw Noah and his sons making Him their priority. Noah's family didn't selfishly hold back any animals, thinking, "We don't have many left." No, after God had safely delivered them from the storm and flood, they wanted to say thank you to God. Their sacrifice probably said to God, "We want fellowship with You." The animal offerings in the Old Testament had many purposes. Some offerings were for transgressions, some for unknown sins, some for worship and some for nothing more than communion with God. Noah's burnt offering could be for all of the above.

"The LORD smelled a sweet savour" (Gen. 8:21, *KJV*) and was pleased. Noah wasn't bringing a sacrifice out of habit. Noah brought a sacrifice because of his relationship with God. Noah brought a sacrifice because he walked with God.

What did God like about the smell? God's enjoyment of the smell was not a selfish thing, like much of our own. We selfishly enjoy the smell of a baking pie. We lie on the lawn to glory in the smell of freshly mown grass or relish how the smell of fresh clean sheets on a bed invites us to sleep.

God smelled the results of Noah's devotion and obedience— and He was pleased. What have you offered to God that would smell sweet to His nose? *Lord, I offer to You my quick obedience.*

God wants to forgive the sin of everyone because He loves the world. He never delights in punishing anyone. When Noah approached God through a blood offering, God was pleased with Noah's obedience when He smelled the smoke of roasted meat on the fire.

Several times in the Old Testament God pointed out that idols of clay or metal "neither see nor hear nor eat nor smell" (Deut. 4:28). Dumb idols do not have the function of personality. Idols can't do anything God can do, so the Eternal Personality enjoyed pointing out their limitation. Idols can't see, nor can they hear the petition of followers. An idol can't even smell the roasted smell of sacrifices offered to it.

When Israel chose to bring sacrifices to God (see Lev. 1–7), on each occasion God was pleased with the smell of the burning sacrifice. God looked beyond what He smelled, and He looked beyond what He saw on the fire. God looked into the hearts of those who offered the sacrifice and was pleased. *Lord, be pleased with my body as a sacrifice to You.*

My Time to Pray

Lord, You were pleased with the sacrifice of Noah
When he presented a burnt offering to You.
Be pleased when I offer my body to You (see Rom. 12:1-2).
Lord, You want me to give everything I have to You;
I surrender all of myself and possessions to You.
Be pleased with what I sacrifice to You.
Amen.

13

God Has Wax in His Ears

The Lord's arm is not too short so He cannot save us,
and His ear is not plugged up with wax so He can't hear us, but our
sins have created a barrier between God and us, and our iniquities
have stopped up His ears, so that He will not hear.
ISAIAH 59:1-2, *AMP*

A worried father had tried everything to get his 16-year-old son to obey him. He had tried bribing his son to cut the grass, but the son was better at the bargaining table than his dad. The son explained, "I need $50 to fill my gas tank." The father paid $50 to get his son to mow the lawn, twice what the lawn service charged.

"Clean up your room," the father yelled. The son yelled back, "It's my room; I can keep it comfortable the way I like."

After many requests to "do this," "do that" and "do as I say" with no response, finally the father prayed, asking God to teach his son some respect and to show the son the error of his ways. But the prayers of the father weren't answered.

"Why doesn't God answer my prayers?" the father said to his preacher on one of his infrequent visits to church. The pastor told the father to keep praying and to pray with all his heart. That was good advice, but not the correct answer. There was a reason why the son was rebellious and why God didn't answer the father's prayer.

In Isaiah 59:2, the prophet states, "Your iniquities have separated you from your God; and your sins have hidden His face from you, so that He will not hear." The father had sin in his life; he had been sleeping around outside marriage. He needed to repent from adultery to get his prayers answered. The father had been too involved with his business when his son was growing up to spend time with his son. The father needed to repent of ignoring his son and begin immediately spending more time with him. The father had not taken responsibility for his chores around the home; he had been too busy with his own life. He needed to repent and invest time at home. No wonder God didn't answer the father's prayers.

In fact, God's ears were plugged up with wax. That's right, wax. The father's sins were like earwax that blocks out hearing. Isaiah 59:1 in the *King James Version* says that God's ear is "heavy." The Hebrew word for "heavy" is the same word used for "blockage." Wax is an external residue that builds up in the ear canal to block sound from reaching the eardrum. Does God hear?

Yes! God has the ability to hear communication from the human voice. God hears everything we say, and God knows everything we think. When we say God has earwax and can't hear us, it means our sins (earwax) are a blockage between God and us.

If God can hear, then does He have ears?

No! God doesn't have ears, eyes or a mouth. God is a spirit and a spirit doesn't have physical organs. When we say "God's ear" that's an anthromorphism (our projection of human organs onto God so we can understand how God does things). Though God is a spirit without a physical body or human organs, He still possesses the abilities these organs provide.

God wants to hear our prayers. He has told us to "Ask, and it will be given to you; seek, and you will find; knock, and it will be opened to you" (Matt. 7:7). Asking is the rule of the Kingdom. It's God's way of keeping His people close to Him.

Just as the physical father in our story is irritated over his son's lack of respect, so too our spiritual Father in heaven has difficulty with His children on earth who will not listen and obey Him. So what are the consequences of our disobedience? Our hypocritical prayers are blocked out because we have sin in our life.

Let's go back and straighten out any misconceptions. Yes, God hears the father's prayer about the rebellious son, because God is omniscient. God knows all things. But the sins of the father have "plugged up" the communication channel between the father and God. That's where we say God's ears are plugged up with wax. God won't do anything about the father's prayers until the father repents and straightens out his life. The father's "changed" lifestyle gives God an avenue to reach the son.

So what does the lesson of earwax tell us about God? Because God is holy, He won't tolerate sin in His followers. When we have sin in our lives, it's the earwax of sin that blocks out our prayers. *Lord, are my sins blocking my prayers?*

God doesn't have to clean out His ears for us to get through. The earwax is our making. We have to confess our sins and repent, which means we yield to Him. We must no longer rebel against God. Then we must begin to do the right thing.

But what about the rebellious son in our story? If God so chooses, He could reach the obstinate teen apart from the spiritually rebellious father. God could use the mother—if she is spiritually concerned—or someone outside the family could influence the son. God could use any number of persons or ways to reach the son, but the sins of the father are the earwax that blocks God's ears to the father's prayers. Perhaps if someone else prays for the rebellious son, God would hear him or her because there is no sin in their life to block God's ears.

The fact that the father is concerned about his son is a starting point. Blocked prayers make us examine ourselves. Why are our prayers not getting through? Earwax is used to get the attention of the father—or any sinning believer—to examine themselves in light of God's standards. *Lord, show me any sin in my life so I can effectively pray.*

The next time you have trouble hearing something or you need to have your ears cleaned out, think of God's ears. Maybe God is having trouble hearing everything you pray because you're responsible for the earwax that's blocking your communication with God. *Lord, forgive my sin and hear my prayers.*

My Time to Pray

Lord, I now realize my prayers are not answered
Because there is sin in my life
That blocks my prayers from reaching You.
Lord, show me any hidden or ignorant sin that blocks
My prayers from reaching You.
I confess to You that I am a sinner;
Forgive me and hear my prayers.
Amen.

14

God Loves to Provide for Our Needs

And Abraham called the name of the place, Jehovah-jireh (The-LORD-Will-Provide); as it is said to this day, "In the Mount of the LORD it shall be provided."
GENESIS 22:14

Early one morning, God called Abraham to go to a mountain that would be shown to him. He was told to offer his son Isaac as a sacrifice to God. We can't spiritualize this command to suggest God wanted Isaac dedicated to God as a living sacrifice. No, the language meant Isaac was to be offered physically as a burnt offering. Some modern translators call it a "whole burnt offering" in which the sacrifice was burned up completely in gratitude or worship of God.

This was an astonishing request. God promised Abraham a son through whom the Messiah would come who would free the world. Also, God promised He would make a great nation through Isaac. Anyone else might have doubted God's request, but Abraham obeyed God and believed that "God was able to raise [Isaac] up from the dead" (Heb. 11:19). And there is another picture to see in this story: the mountain to which God would lead Abraham is the same mountain where the fulfillment of God's ultimate plan would take place, the mountain where Jesus would eventually be crucified and die.

When God called Abraham, the old patriarch answered, "Here I am," showing his obedience to God (Gen. 22:1). Here is where

Abraham became a man of faith and because of it, God called him His friend (see Isa. 41:8; 2 Chron. 20:7). Later in the New Testament, James writes, "And the Scripture was fulfilled which says, *'Abraham believed God, and it was accounted to him for righteousness,'* And he was called the friend of God" (Jas. 2:23).

When Abraham and Isaac got to the top of the mountain, the young Isaac asked, "Look, the fire and the wood, but where is the lamb for a burnt offering?" (Gen. 22:7).

The father answered prophetically, "My son, God will provide for Himself the lamb for a burnt offering" (Gen. 22:8). Abraham's answer provides a prediction of the substitution death of Christ who died for us.

When Abraham lifted his arm with knife in hand to take the life of his son, God called him by name, "Abraham, Abraham" (Gen. 22:11). With the same obedience that he began the journey, Abraham again answered, "Here I am" (Gen. 22:11).

Because of his obedience, God provided the sacrificial animal. Abraham saw a ram caught in thick vines by its horns (so it could be unblemished). Abraham offered the ram as a whole burnt offering of praise and worship to God and named the place Jehovah-jireh, which means "God supplies."

We can learn two lessons from this event. First, on this mountain God "provided Himself" as the sacrificial lamb who died for the sins of the world. Calvary is "Jehovah-jireh," the place God provided salvation for all. *Lord, thank You for providing for my salvation.*

The second lesson is that God will provide for us. But we must be careful when we ask for God's provision. Don't be like the lazy ministerial student who said he was trusting God to provide his finances when in actuality he was lazy, didn't work for money and didn't really intercede that deeply. He had empty faith when claiming "Jehovah-jireh."

The China Inland Mission was the first great Faith Foreign Mission Board. Some of the greatest and godliest missionaries evangelized inland China without a guaranteed salary, trusting God to supply all their financial needs. Over the door to their headquarters in England was written their motto, "Jehovah-jireh."

God loves to provide for His people, but notice that His provision is based on *relationship*. Just as Abraham obeyed, so too you must obey if you want God's provision.

Abraham was surrendered to God. He was willing to go where God led, and he ventured out not knowing where he was going. He began his journey with the attitude, "Here I am." *Lord, here I am to do Your will.*

Abraham followed the Lord on a three-day excursion. Abraham did not make a spur of the moment act of surrender to God. Abraham had made a lifetime commitment. For God to provide for you, you must also make a long-term commitment. You must pray, *Lord, I will go where You lead me.*

Abraham was asked to do one of the most difficult things in life. He was asked to sacrifice his dreams. Don't most fathers have great dreams for their son? Abraham was asked to sacrifice his love. And if his son were gone, everything he valued in life would be destroyed. But Abraham received everything God promised him because he was willing to give up everything. *Lord, I give You everything; I give You my life.*

My Time to Pray

Lord, I trust my entire life to You.
I know You will protect me
And You will provide what You promise.
I surrender my entire life to You;
Take me and use me according to Your will.
Lord, I worship You as Jehovah-jireh.
I wait silently in Your presence.
Amen.

15

God's Eyes See All

For the eyes of the LORD are on the righteous,
and His ears are open to their prayers.
1 PETER 3:12

The church was packed on Mother's Day, so all the family couldn't sit together. The mother sat with the youngest child in front of the father, who was attempting to hold his toddler son, a hyperactive and playful child.

The whole church sang a familiar hymn, "This is my Father's world, and to His listening ears . . ." Little John had learned a comic song in kindergarten that involved putting his hands behind his ears and waving them.

"John, put your hands down," Mother said from her seat without looking around. She knew what her son was doing.

Later during the sermon, little John stood behind his mother; no one noticed he was standing because he was so short. He examined his mother's hair carefully without touching it. He looked at it from the left . . . right . . . and bottom. Finally he parted her hair, at which she turned around and made him sit down.

At home, mother asked in exasperation what he was doing with her hair. "I was looking for your eyes in the back of your head." Because Mother had caught him doing so many things when she wasn't looking, little John heard she had eyes in the back of her head.

Did you know God has eyes?

He does, although they are not in the back of His head. As a matter of fact, God doesn't have literal eyes. The "eyes of the Lord" is a metaphor to help us understand the personhood of God. We need eyes to see things so we can know them. God knows all things but without the necessity of physical eyes.

God's knowing is called omniscience. He knows all things—past, present and future—both actual and potential. He knows all things without effort; God doesn't have to strain to remember as we do. God never forgets. *Lord, You know everything about me. You know all my needs.*

God knows all things because He is omnipresent, equally present everywhere all the time. Since He is everywhere, He knows everything that's happening. *Lord, You know all the good things I do, and the times I disobey.*

God even knows things about people that you can't know. You can't know people's thoughts. You may know their actions, but you don't know what your friends are thinking. But God knows. "O Lord, You . . . know everything about me . . . You know my every thought . . . You know what I am going to say before I even say it" (Ps. 139:1-2,4, *TLB*).

Yes, God has eyes to know us, but His eyes are a metaphor. God doesn't have blue eyes or brown eyes, but God has all-knowing eyes. Because God's eyes see all we do, the verse at the beginning of this chapter says He is open to hear our prayers. God knows if we are sincere, and God knows if we are honestly trying to keep His commandments. *Lord, see my sincere effort and hear my prayers.*

What do God's eyes see? He sees our actions, our thoughts, our dreams, our good and our sin. The Lord sees the evil of people's hearts. "The face of the Lord is against those who do evil . . ." (Ps. 34:16). That ought to be a warning to all. The fact that God has eyes to see ought to influence us when we pray. Not one of us is without sin, but in the integrity of our hearts, we can have, like Paul, "a conscience, void of offense to God" (Acts 24:16). *Lord, forgive my sin that You see in me.*

The Lord's ability to see goes beyond His believers. The Lord sees everything in every person. "For the eyes of the Lord run to and fro throughout the whole earth . . ." (2 Chron. 16:9). There's no place where people can hide from the Lord. His eyes see everything. "I can never get away from my God! . . . even darkness cannot hide from God . . ." (Ps. 139:7,12, *TLB*). *Lord, shine Your face on my life; forgive my sins and keep me from evil.*

Also, don't count on the Lord missing your sins because He is sleeping. God sees everything, all the time, because He never sleeps. "He will never let me stumble, slip or fall. For He is always watching, never sleeping" (Ps. 121:4, *TLB*).

My Time to Pray

Lord, I take comfort in Your all-seeing eyes.
You see and know all I do and think;
Forgive me when I slip or commit a presumptuous sin.
Cleanse my heart from hypocrisy.
Lord, because You see all I do,
I come to You with a humble heart,
Asking for mercy and forgiveness.
Hear my heart's prayers, and give me the prayers
That are asked within Your will.
Amen.

16

God Hates Certain Things

*These six [things] the LORD hates, yes, seven [are] an abomination to
Him: A proud look, a lying tongue, hands that shed innocent blood, a
heart that devises wicked plans, feet that are swift in running to evil, a false
witness [who] speaks lies, and one who sows discord among brethren.*
PROVERBS 6:16-19

We often hear about God's love, but God is capable of hate too.
Look again at the opening verse from Proverbs that lists what
God hates. First, it's a proud look. Certain people have that selfish glow when they are pleased with themselves or they have
gained mastery of others.

The second thing God hates is a lying tongue, and the third
thing He hates are hands that shed innocent blood. The fourth
thing is people with wicked dreams and imaginations because
people usually act out dreams they imagine.

The fifth thing God hates are feet that are quick to run to
do mischief. The mischief here is harm to people.

The sixth thing that God hates is a proud heart that becomes a false witness who spreads lies. Most selfish people are
blind to the good things of others. They exalt themselves and
believe the lies they tell about themselves. Then they put others
down and believe the lies and rumors they spread about others.

The seventh thing the Lord hates is the one sowing discord among other Christians. If you love other people, you wouldn't spread rumors that destroy them.

These seven things that God hates deal with inward sins of the heart, not outward sins. Our inward motives always determine our outward actions; our inward selfish pride is the source of our sin that God hates.

Notice that our selfishness is the basis for several things the Lord hates, such as pride, false witnesses, lies and sowing discord among friends. When a man or woman is all bound up in a selfish lifestyle, they can't worship or serve the Lord. The Lord hates it when something gets in the way of worship.

Most people don't like selfish individuals. Who likes to listen to a guy who always talks about his accomplishments, possessions and interest? Who wants to spend time with a woman who is only concerned with her looks, clothes and what she does to have a fun time?

It's not wrong to talk about your accomplishments, if you do it at the right time for the right reason. And it's not wrong to be concerned about your clothes and the way you dress. There is a place for self-love. Remember the Great Commandment: "You shall love the LORD your God with all your heart . . . soul, and . . . mind" (Matt. 22:37-38). Don't forget the second part: "You shall love your neighbor as yourself" (Matt. 22:39). Did you see that part about "love yourself"? God recognizes our self-love.

God knew it was natural for people to love themselves or He wouldn't have added "as you love yourself." So how is it all right to love oneself? Let's call it "self-respect." We must know ourselves for who we are. It's all right to feel the satisfaction of accomplishment when we do well. It's wrong to brag about our accomplishments that are greater than they really are. That's lying, or worse, self-worship. That's where the ego comes in; that's where sin influences us.

It's not wrong to love yourself properly with self-worth or self-respect. If we exaggerate our self-worth, that's pride. But if we minimize our self-worth, we create low self-esteem. So what's a healthy ego or a proper self-esteem? It's when we know ourselves for who we are. It's when we don't exaggerate or diminish our self-worth. It's when we're honest with our self.

When Jesus came, He announced that the Kingdom of heaven was a spiritual kingdom where He desired to sit on the throne of our hearts, to rule our life. Who controls your heart and life?

When selfish pride sits on the throne of your life, Christ is displaced. You can't call Him Lord and give Him second place in your life. *Lord, come now, and sit on the throne of my heart.*

But let's not end on a negative factor; let's look again at God's love that is everlasting and His mercy that forgives every sin our selfish pride conceives. Let's praise God for the cross for that's where the blood of Christ was poured out for the forgiveness of sin. *Lord, thank You for Your grace and mercy You brought through the cross.*

My Time to Pray

Lord, thank You that in mercy You have forgiven me;
I claim Your cleansing by the blood of Christ.
Forgive me for my pride and selfish acts,
That exalted me and not You.
Lord, help me be honest about myself
And my accomplishments.
Help me exalt Christ in all I do,
Then I won't have trouble with pride.
Amen.

17

God Heals Protectively

If you diligently heed the voice of the Lord your God and do what is right in His sight, give ear to His commandments and keep all His statutes, I will put none of the diseases on you which I have brought on the Egyptians. For I am the Lord (Jehovah Rapha) who heals you.
EXODUS 15:26

In the Bible, we see that God is concerned about our health and healing. The Lord can bring healing in two ways. The first is preventative healing by keeping disease and bacteria from infecting us. The second is through curative medicine that makes us well when we are sick. We can pray for the Lord to actively heal us.

In a small way, a mother provides these same forms of healing for her children. To prevent her child from getting sick, a mother will make sure the home is clean, disinfecting and getting rid of as many germs as possible. She'll make sure her child gets well-balanced healthy meals. When the child goes out in cold weather, she will make sure he is dressed properly. And oh, don't forget the shots. She makes sure he is vaccinated.

But we live in a germ-infected world, and most every child will catch a cold or virus. That's where curative medicine comes in. A loving mother takes the child's temperature and spoons out medicine. She phones the doctor and makes sure her child gets an antibiotic. She puts him to bed and makes sure the child gets rest and sleep. She does everything to cure the illness and make him well.

Just like the mother, God has compassion for His children. He wants us to live healthy lives of worship and service. God never planned to save the souls of His children and neglect their physical bodies.

God wanted His people to be holy, which involved being clean in their speech, their clothing and their bodies. So God instructed His children how to live, and those who obey His instruction are kept from many of the diseases that attack the body.

When Christians said they wouldn't smoke tobacco products, many laughed at them, accusing Christians of being legalistic or judgmental. But medical research later proved that smoking leads to lung cancer and other diseases. Since the body of a believer is the temple of the Holy Spirit, God wants the body clean because He lives in the believer. So separation from sin has proven to be God's preventative healing.

The same is true with drinking alcohol to get drunk. God wants His people to be in control of their mental and physical faculties, and when they get drunk, they lose control. Also, alcohol consumption can lead to cirrhosis of the liver, hardening of the arteries and a host of other diseases. Shakespeare said, "He who fills his stomach with wine destroys his mind."

Think of all the dietary restrictions God put upon His people in the wilderness. They couldn't eat certain reptiles, birds or insects. They couldn't even eat fish that didn't have scales. God was not being arbitrary. One thing characterized all the living things they couldn't eat: they were all scavenger animals.

Think of all the germs in a dead carcass or the bacteria found in a garbage dump. Some of the prohibited animals ate the highly germ-infested feces of other animals. God didn't want His people to put an animal into their bodies that was filled with germs and poison. The animals they could eat were vegetarians.

Even God's rule of sexual purity (abstinence) was preventative health. There is a worldwide epidemic of AIDS and its corollary diseases. Governments are spending billions to find a cure for this deadly disease, but AIDS could be mostly wiped out if every man and woman obeyed God's commands, "Thou shalt not commit adultery" (Exod. 20:14, *KJV*) and "Flee fornication" (1 Cor. 6:18, *KJV*). *Lord, I will be sexually pure; be glorified in my body.*

You serve the Lord who is *Jehovah Rapha*—the Lord that Heals. He blesses your life with preventative medicine, but to be healthy, you have a responsibility to "listen to the voice of the Lord your God" (Exod. 15:26). More than just knowing God's rules for healthy living, you must "keep all His principles" (Exod. 15:26).

When you know the Lord and love Him with all your heart, then you want to please Him in every area of your life. You want to be holy in your thoughts, and holy in your emotions. When you are holy and clean in your inner life, it's only natural you'll be holy in your outward physical life.

So live a life of worship. Just as the Old Testament saints worshiped God by bringing a lamb in sacrificial worship, so too you can worship God with a living sacrifice. The Bible instructs us how to do this: "I beseech you therefore, brethren, by the mercies of God, that you present your bodies a living sacrifice, holy, acceptable to God, which is your reasonable service" (Rom. 12:1). Your holiness—cleanliness—is worship to God.

By worshiping God with your body, you are taking steps toward preventative health. You allow Him to be *Jehovah Rapha* to you.

My Time to Pray

Lord, forgive me when I complain about Your commands;
At times I think I know better than You.
Help me see the big picture that You have
For my inward holiness and outward health.
Forgive me when I disobey Your commands,
And sin in either my heart or with my body.
Protect me from disease that attacks my body;
Heal me; make me healthy to serve You.
Lord, I worship You for Your goodness and care.
Thank You for Your wise commands to make me healthy.
Amen.

18

God Laughs

"Likewise, I [Jesus] say unto you, God gets happy in Heaven in the presence of His angels over one lost sinner that repents."
LUKE 15:10, *AMP*

"Do you hear that?" The man said cupping his hand behind his ear. "I'd recognize that laugh anywhere." They were standing at the opening into a valley, but they couldn't see into the valley as it was night. The voice was coming toward him up the valley, and it was not yelling for help. It was laughing.

The valley was desolate, a place no one would visit after dark. There were steep rocks and dangerous pits. If you fell in one, there was no escape. Black openings to threatening caves concealed unknown hungry predators lurking within.

"Listen," the man said, "you can hear him clearly, and it's a happy voice."

Walking up the valley came a shepherd with a sheep on his shoulder. His laughter was infectious; you wanted to laugh with him. "Rejoice with me, I have found my sheep."

At sundown the shepherd had been tired from chasing stray sheep in the hot sun. He was looking forward to a hot meal and the rest of sleep. But he didn't eat first. He constantly circled his flock looking for snakes, alkaline water or poisonous roots. His sheep were gullible; they had no sense of danger.

As the sun was setting the shepherd began a small fire to cook a simple meal and rest. "Soon I can sleep," he thought. He called his sheep by name, and most obeyed to enter the sheepfold. Then the shepherd called a name of a rebellious sheep, one that had difficulty obeying.

No movement in the flock; no response. The sheep didn't come.

The shepherd circled the flock again, looking for any telltale evidence of the rebellious one. The rebellious sheep could not be seen. With panic the shepherd rapidly gathered all the flock into the sheepfold. It was a rock wall enclosure that was overgrown with thorns and thistles—to keep sheep in and predators out.

The shepherd called the name again, but no answer. Then he carefully counted . . . 97 . . . 98 . . . 99 . . . one missing.

The shepherd would never say, "Serves him right for running away!" Nor would the shepherd eat his hot meal and get some needed sleep. No! He left his other sheep locked safe in their pen to go searching immediately for his lost sheep. A good shepherd would sacrifice his comfort, not thinking of his tired body. He would face the dangers of the night to find one lost sheep. Why would he do that? Love! Shepherds love their sheep.

Jesus told this Parable of the Lost Sheep in Matthew 18:12-14 and Luke 15:3-7. His listeners, many of whom might have been shepherds themselves, would have understood the imagery and the point that Jesus was making. Today, few of us are as familiar with shepherding, so the depiction might be a bit tougher for us to grasp. But all of us can understand the sacrifices a mother makes for her baby. All us have seen a pet owner cry when burying his or her beloved dog or cat. All of us can understand love. God loves sinners and has gone to unfathomable lengths to rescue them. Angels worshiped Jesus and did His bidding in heaven but Jesus gave up the comforts of heaven to come to earth. He came not to be served, but to serve and sacrifice His life as a ransom for all. He came seeking lost sheep. *Thank You, Jesus, for coming to find me.*

Because Jesus lived a perfect life without sin, men who were sinners hated Him, ridiculed Him and condemned Him to death. They crushed a crown of thorns on His head and beat Him viciously with a cat-o'-nine-tails whip. When He had no strength left, they forced Him to carry a cross—the instrument of execution—up a hill called Calvary. They laid Him upon that cross and drove spikes through His hands and feet. They stood the cross in the blazing sun and left Him to die.

Jesus the shepherd died for His sheep of this world. Why? Because He loved them. Because they were lost. Because they couldn't help themselves. *Lord, I bow in utter amazement.*

The sheep of this world are gullible; they have no sense of danger. They eat, sleep and do the things they want to do, not realizing how close danger lurks. Why did Jesus die for this adrift bunch? Because He loves them.

Listen to the laughter! Jesus the shepherd is coming with another sheep that He has rescued. He's laughing as He carries the sheep on His shoulder. Listen as He shouts to us, "Rejoice with me for I have found my sheep which was lost" (Luke 15:6).

Why does Jesus laugh? The salvation of a lost person makes Him happy. There's not much in the Bible that describes God's laughing except His rejoicing over lost people being saved: "Likewise, I (Jesus) say unto you, God gets happy in Heaven in the presence of His angels over one lost sinner that repents" (Luke 15:10, *AMP*).

What makes you the happiest in life? And with whom do you celebrate when you are happiest? If you get a pay raise, do you celebrate with fellow workers? With your spouse? With a best friend? Apparently, God celebrates with the angels. *Lord, thank You for rejoicing over me in front of the angels.*

You can tell a lot about a person from the things that make him or her happy. Since we are made in the image of God, we should have the same likes and dislikes as God. Winning souls makes God happier than anything else because creating man was greater to God than creating the universe. Creation was the greatest thing God did until the birth of the Christ child to a virgin in Bethlehem. Greater yet was Jesus dying on the cross for mankind—and greater than that was Jesus being raised from the dead to give life.

No wonder God laughs with enjoyment when someone is saved!

My Time to Pray

Lord, thank You for coming to earth to seek lost sheep;
Thank You for seeking me when I was lost.
Thank You for rescuing me from sin's danger,
And giving me salvation from sin.
Lord, I rejoice with You, for the Bible says, "You laugh"
When someone is saved.
I laugh with You because I was one who was saved.
I was lost but now I am found.
Amen.

19

God Gets Weary

Jesus therefore, being wearied from His journey, sat thus by the well.
JOHN 4:6

You have wearied Me with your iniquities.
ISAIAH 43:24

The April sun was merciless, and each hill between Jerusalem and Samaria was monotonously ruthless. Jesus was worn out from pulling Himself up one hill after another. Going down was not even easy for it took muscles to hold one back from running.

Jesus and His disciples were returning from the Feast of Passover in Jerusalem in the spring of AD 27. Jesus had decided to not go by way of the Jordan River valley that was easy and relatively flat. Jesus had decided to go cross-country through Samaria, a hilly path.

Finally up ahead they saw a narrow valley through the hills. It went between Mount Gerizim and Mount Ebal, mountains famous to every Jew for they were the Mount of Blessings and the Mount of Cursings. But it wasn't the valley or the mountains they anticipated. It was the well of Jacob in the valley. The day was hot, the journey was long and they looked forward to cool water.

"Less than a mile to go," Peter announced to the tired disciples. They had been pushing themselves to get through Samaria since no respecting Jew wanted to be stuck in Samaritan territory overnight. The Jews wanted nothing to do with the people they called "the Samaritan half-breeds." They were all hoping to make it to Galilee by nightfall. There they could enjoy a Jewish meal and Jewish hospitality. If they could not make it to Galilee, they would have to sleep on the ground around a campfire since no conscientious Jew would sleep in a Samaritan home.

"Let me help you," Peter said as he put a strong arm around Jesus to help Him make it the last few steps to the well. John thought to himself, *Jesus couldn't have gone a step further.*

Jesus slumped onto a stone wall in the shade. He was tired and weary. The rest would replenish His spirit, and water would renew His body.

Jesus laid His head against a tree and fell sound asleep. The disciples decided to let Jesus rest while they went into the nearby town of Sychar to get some food to eat.

Did you see what happened there? Jesus got tired. Just like you and me, Jesus experienced fatigue. He knew what it was like to face exhaustion and relish in the renewal of rest.

Don't forget the time He fell asleep in the boat crossing the Sea of Galilee. He had preached all morning and was tired. The breeze on the lake and the soft lapping waves on the boat put a tired Jesus to sleep. *Lord I forget that You were human, that You understand my tiredness.*

Even though Jesus was unlimited throughout eternity and was the omnipotent God, when He was born as a babe, He took on the limitations of human flesh. It is said a man will die if he goes seven days without water, and Jesus' body was no different.

He needed water, so He asked a Samaritan woman, "Give me a drink" (John 4:7). Jesus had to eat to keep His strength; He did not perform a miracle to get food.

When Jesus was on earth, He got physically tired from walking, preaching and healing in the hot climate of the Holy Land. He got tired because He was fully man. *Lord, thank You for becoming a man for me.*

Even though Jesus was also fully the God of the ages, when He came to the world, He took on a human body that got tired. God the Father doesn't need rest, nor does He need refreshing, but Jesus, the man, got tired. This trip from Jerusalem through Samaria seemed to tire Him out more than at other times.

Being tired means being pushed to the limits of one's endurance. Though God doesn't need rest, is it possible for Him to be pushed to the limits of His endurance by our sin.

God says, "You have wearied Me with your iniquities" (Isa. 43:24). God doesn't get physically tired or exhausted, but God can get weary dealing with our sins. The verse from Isaiah demonstrates that our sins push God to the limits of His patience. *Lord, I'm sorry for making You tired.*

Fortunately, God is patient with our sins because He loves us. But God will not withhold His punishment forever. When He's wearied with our sins, He releases His judgment to punish sin.

Notice how patient Jesus was with the woman at the well. She was spiritually blind to the message of Jesus, but He gave her the most irresistible offer: "If you knew the gift of God, and who it is who says to you, 'Give Me a drink,' you would have asked Him, and He would have given you living water" (John 4:26). The answer to the woman's sin was Jesus Christ. He's your answer too.

Next time you get so tired that all you can do is sit down or lie down, remember that Jesus also got tired in this life. The next time you persistently sin, remember God's warning: "You have wearied Me with your iniquities" (Isa. 43:24). Remember: Jesus is the friend of sinners. *Lord, I came to You; there's no place else I can go.*

Jesus invites you, "Come to me, all of you who are weary and carry heavy burdens, and I will give you rest. Take my yoke upon you. Let me teach you, because I am humble and gentle at heart, and you will find rest for your souls. For my yoke is easy to bear, and the burden I give you is light" (Matt. 11:28-30, *NLT*).

My Time to Pray

Lord, I've never realized that You get weary,
That You get tired of my sin.
I'm sorry for any pain I've caused You,
And I'm sorry for my selfish disobedience.
Lord, forgive my insensitive reaction to You;
My sins have wearied You and I didn't know it.
Forgive my sins and forget about my disobedience.
I will obey Your words and commands.
I want to please You.
Amen.

20

God Gets Angry

The LORD avenges and [is] furious. The LORD will take vengeance on His adversaries, And He reserves [wrath] for His enemies; the LORD [is] slow to anger.
NAHUM 1:2-3

A young single mom was perpetually angry. Her husband divorced her because she always fussed at him. She was mad at life because she got stuck with a baby. She barely got through high school, hated to study and never acquired a skill for a job. She ended up as a maid, cleaning motel rooms. She hated her job, as evidenced by her messy apartment that smelled because she never cleaned it up.

Her bank card and department store bills were several months delinquent. The collection agency phoned over and over again about the overdue bills. When one creditor threatened further action, she mailed a check for more than $400 to satisfy the immediate problem. However, the creditor phoned her again because the store never received the check.

The single mother went into a rage. She insisted the store was "dumb" for losing her check, and blamed the store for not hiring enough people to take care of business correctly.

When the agent on the phone asked if she had mailed the check after writing it, she yelled at him again. He tactfully suggested that she might have lost the envelope. He asked her to look in the drawer where she kept her bills or in her purse.

The woman continued to yell. Next, she blamed the post office. Now she was angry at the post office for not delivering the check to the store! Eventually, she settled down long enough to call her bank and cancel the check. Still griping and complaining, she mailed the second check for the balance to the store. Everyone who knew the single mom knew her anger was destroying her life, financially, socially and emotionally, but the woman continued to rage on, unaware of the vast impact her anger was having on her.

Did you know that God gets angry? He has standards of holiness, and when people break His laws or principles, He becomes angry at their sin. So, if God gets angry, then it must be all right for us to get angry, right? Yes—but we must get angry at the right thing and for the right reason. It's wrong to get angry at the wrong person or for the wrong reason. The Bible instructs us, "Be angry, and do not sin" (Eph. 4:26). This verse allows us to be angry, but it warns us not to sin with our anger.

We get our anger from God because we are made in the image of God, which means we have His nature. In the perfect world, only the things that anger God would anger us, but we are fallen, sinful beings and so our anger often is expressed in inappropriate ways and times. God gave us the Ten Commandments to tell us how to live. The order of the 10 laws reflects their importance. The First Commandment tells us to have no gods before Him. The Second Commandment tells us not to have any carved idols. Those who bow down to idols are warned, "I, the LORD your God, [am] a jealous God, visiting the iniquity of the fathers on the children to the third and fourth [generations] of those who hate Me" (Exod. 20:5). Did you see why God gets angry? Those who worship an idol instead of God hate Him.

Because God created us and we belong to Him, we make Him angry when we refuse to recognize His lordship over us. God gets angry when we put something in the place of God. *Lord, I put You first in my life.*

Compare God's anger to the illustration of the single mom's anger. God shows His anger only at the right time, for the right reason. God doesn't walk around angry at every person. In contrast, the single mom was angry at everyone and blamed everyone for her problems.

Though God gets angry, He doesn't always act on it. God controls His anger. The Bible tells us that "The LORD [is] slow to anger" (Nah. 1:3). If He instantly punished everyone who broke His law, no one would live; all would be eliminated from the face of the earth. *Lord, thank You for Your patience with me.*

What holds God back from immediately punishing every sin and every sinner? It's His everlasting love for people. God is able to control His anger because of His compassion.

Perhaps the single mom has never truly learned love. Maybe she's never been loved, so she is not able to love others. Maybe she's angry because no one cares for her and protects her from the uncertainties of life.

Remember, God loves you and has a wonderful plan for your life. As God progressively leads you, He is showing you His love. So find God's plan for your life and do it. *Lord, I want Your plan for my life.*

My Time to Pray

Lord, sometimes I'm angry at the wrong person
For the wrong reason; forgive me.
Help me control my temper and anger;
Give me the Holy Spirit's power to do it.
Lord, I need to be transformed by Your power;
I need to live like Christ.
Amen.

21

God Waits

*Therefore the L*ORD *will wait, that He may be gracious to you; and therefore He will be exalted . . . blessed are all those who wait for Him.*
ISAIAH 30:18

We (Charles and Elmer) have different temperaments when it comes to waiting, whether it's waiting in a long line of shoppers, or waiting when we're caught in traffic gridlock. Charles is fairly easygoing. He knows there is not much he can do with long lines. So, in the car he listens to some praise worship CDs, or if he's waiting for a delayed airplane, he listens to his iPod.

I (Elmer), on the other hand, am impatient. It's not that I get irritated with someone who wastes my time or frustrated with a traffic jam. What irks me is the feeling that I'm missing out on doing something profitable. I'm good with time management. I've got my day planned and my desk organized so I can get as much done as possible. I don't like to wait because I feel I'm wasting time. When external forces hold me back, I get impatient because I think of all I could be doing for God. So when I do have to wait, I pray.

Have you ever thought that God has to wait? Most of us think that God is all-powerful, so He doesn't have to wait. He just makes everything happen on His schedule. But the Bible teaches that God waits. Why does God wait and how does He deal with it?

God has purpose when He is waiting. He waits for people to repent of sin and turn to Him. He doesn't immediately judge every sin they commit; He gives people an opportunity to turn to Him.

God knows all things. He knows those who will get saved and those who won't. Time does not constrain God. He lives in the past, present and future. Right now God is present at the day of every person's salvation. He knows those who will not believe, but gives them a complete calendar of pre-determined days. Then, God waits.

Sometimes, even though God answers our prayers immediately, we have to wait to see the fruit of His response. When we beg God for money for our church, He doesn't instantly make cash appear. Instead when we pray, God touches the heart of someone to give money. But then there are the logistical steps that have to take place: the person has to write a check and mail it. Sometimes the person neglects to go swiftly to the mailbox, and sometimes the mail is delayed. Even though we may think that God has answered "No," in actuality we just have to be patient to allow God's process to work. The same process happens when you pray for healing. Suppose you ask God to heal someone. They don't usually spring immediately out of bed and go back to work. Health and strength come slowly. Suppose God healed instantly by taking away a germ or infection. Doesn't it take time for infection to be flushed out of the bodily systems? Maybe the sick person needs sleep to get their strength back, or they need food to get their health back. God heals, then sits back and waits for healing to strengthen the whole body.

Jeremiah reminds us that God promises: "I bring upon them all the good that I have promised them" (Jer. 32:42). God has good plans for our life. But most of us have some rebellion and we don't follow God in every small way that we should. So God can't give us the good things He promises. God has to work His good plan for us through detours and some side excursions. God waits to give us good things. *Thank You, Lord, for waiting with patience.*

God wants to use us, but we're not always spiritual enough or prepared enough. My (Elmer's) first sermon was a flop. I preached on a street corner in Columbia, South Carolina, to about four or five soldiers and two students from Columbia Bible College. I preached about three minutes and ran out of stuff to say, so I repeated my sermon in two minutes. I gave an invitation and nothing happened. God couldn't use me; I wasn't ready to be used by God. He had to wait until I became more mature.

In the same way, God waits for each of us to become mature enough in our faith so that He can use us for His purposes. He is patient, and He will work with us and develop us until we can be used for the plans that He has in store for us. *Lord, thank You for not giving up on us.*

My Time to Pray

Lord, patience is one of Your attributes;
Thank You for being patient with me.
Lord, if You judged every sin immediately,
I would not last long on this earth.
Lord, I need patience to be more like You.
Teach me when to wait patiently
And when to stubbornly push ahead.
Amen.

22

God Whistles

He raises a signal flag for the distant nations
and whistles for them from the ends of the earth.
Look—how quickly and swiftly they come!
ISAIAH 5:26, CSB

My wife and I (Elmer) fell in love at Columbia Bible College in the early 50s. The school had rules for couples going steady that prevented them from spending too much time together. You were allowed two dates a week, and we could chat briefly in the halls between classes. But there was no endless hanging out like young couples are prone to do.

I worked in the school kitchen in a variety of jobs. One of them was breakfast set-up, which included putting out milk, juice and cereals, and making coffee.

Ruth lived on the fourth floor of the women's dorm; her windows were right over the door I entered into the kitchen every morning.

I arrived each morning around 5:45 AM. Usually everything was quiet. No street noise and no activity in the dorms. When I approached the dorm, I'd whistle "I Dream of Jeanie with the Light Brown Hair." The light would go on, the shades would roll up and there she was at the window to wave at me. Her middle name was Jean, so I had a certain affinity for the song.

My morning whistle was a signal to her, which allowed us a few more seconds of interaction each day. Even though we couldn't talk, that was a special time together. I could feel my emotions running as I got close to the kitchen door.

A whistle is a signal.

When I went to cowboy movies as a kid, one of my favorite Wild West heroes signaled for his horse with a whistle. A boy whistles for his dog to come. Construction workers whistle a signal to one another. And don't we whistle our approval for a home run, touchdown or winning basket?

My mother used to whistle for me (Elmer) when I was out playing in the neighborhood. Along about sundown she would come to the back porch, lean over the banister toward the place I was playing, put her fingers in her mouth and whistle the loudest signal in our neighborhood. Our neighborhood was two blocks across and five blocks long, so I could hear her anywhere I played.

Her whistle was an invitation, a signal that supper was on the table. I always came running when she called because what she had on the table was better than any game I could play. There was always a home-cooked meal waiting: meat, potatoes, three or four vegetables out of our garden and a big glass of iced tea, already sweetened. This was mother's happiest time of day for she loved to see us enjoy our meal, almost as much as she enjoyed cooking it.

Did you know that God whistles when He wants to signal Israel to come home? One day in the future, God will go out on the back porch of heaven, lean over the banister of paradise and whistle for His children—Israel—to come home to the Promised Land. From all over the earth the Jews will return to the land that will flow with milk and honey. "He will lift up a banner to the Gentile nations, and will whistle to His people who are in the ends of the earth. They shall come speedily" (Isa. 5:26, *AMP*). And what son of Abraham could stay away when God whistles for him to come home?

And when they return, look at the smile on God's face. And just like my mother, who reveled in people eating her home cooking almost as much as preparing the meal, God will have fulfilled His promises. He will smile as His people Israel come home to supper.

God's whistle tells us three things. First, God keeps His Word. God promised to Abraham (see Gen. 12:7), Isaac (see Gen. 26:3) and Jacob (see Gen. 35:12) that He would give the land of Israel to their descendants. God's whistle signals that He is keeping His promise and giving them the promise land.

Second, God is whistling for His people to come home to rest and peace. For thousands of years the Jews have been persecuted, but when God whistles for them, they will be coming home to peace.

Third, God's whistle means it's the end. Just as my mother whistled for me to stop playing and come home at the end of a day, so too God whistles at the end of the Dispensation of the Gentiles. His whistle begins the Millennial Age for the Jews.

But we saved Gentiles are not waiting for a whistle. We're waiting for a shout from heaven. It will be Jesus calling us to meet Him in the air. "For the Lord He shall descend from heaven with a shout . . . and the dead in Christ will rise first. Then we who are alive and remain shall be caught up together with them in the clouds to meet the Lord in the air; and so shall we ever be with the Lord" (1 Thess. 4:16-17).

Honestly though, we don't care what we hear, whether it's a whistle or a shout; we're looking for a person. We're waiting for Jesus. *Lord, I'm listening.*

My Time to Pray

Lord, a whistle can be a good thing.
I whistle when I'm glad or amazed.
I whistle my joy and worship to You.
Lord, be blessed with my worship
that comes from my heart.
Be pleased when I worship You sincerely.
Amen.

23

God Anguishes

*Then Jesus came with them (the disciples) into a garden
called Gethsemane . . . then Jesus said to them, "My soul is
anguished even to death; wait and pray with me."*
MATTHEW 26:36,38, *AMP*

*And being in agony, he anguished in prayer,
and great drops of blood, as sweat, fell to the ground.*
LUKE 22:44, *AMP*

Shrouded by dark clouds looming in the east, the moon refused to show itself. The apostles struggled to distinguish the garden path by starlight.

"If the Master did not come here so often," Thomas said, "we would never find the garden in the darkness."

They knew the way because they came often with Jesus to pray in the Garden of Gethsemane. Now He strode toward the garden without a misstep, even as the apostles stumbled over stones and tree roots, unable to see the ground in front of them. Each was lost in his own thoughts, haunted by Jesus' dire predictions that each of them would forsake Him before the night was through.

The city of Jerusalem slept silently behind them. Water gurgled in the creek of Kidron below them. The April rains had freshened the springs, and the lapping brook was the only sound that broke the silence of the night.

Off to their right appeared the vague silhouettes of a grove of olive trees. Because their gnarled trunks made for excellent seats, Jesus directed the apostles, "Sit here," as they entered the garden. "I will go ahead to pray."

He took Peter, James and John with Him, disappearing into the darkness. It was late in the evening, and the apostles were tired and growing cold. They wrapped their tunics about them to ward off the damp chill. Soon they were sleeping propped against the olive trees.

Deeper in the garden, Jesus spoke to His three closest disciples, clearly in anguish. "I am overwhelmed with grief," He said, "crushed almost to the point of death."

Jesus instructed the three, "Stay here and keep watch with me as I pray." But even as Jesus walked away, the three men felt their eyes growing heavy and their shoulders sagging.

About a stone's throw away, Jesus fell to His knees to pray. Visions of the cross bore down on Him; He knew the intense pain and agony that awaited Him on the morrow. He cried out to His Father as the darkness pressed in on His Spirit from all sides. "*My Father . . .*" the words poured from Jesus' heart like water from a pitcher . . . "*if it is possible, I don't want to drink this cup of suffering.*"

Jesus' agony was so intense that He could no longer remain on His knees. He fell with His face to the ground . . . His fists clenched . . . His voice tightened. He repeated His plea: "*Father, if You are willing, please take this cup from Me.*"

The garden usually talked to Him at night. Jesus often heard the hoot of an owl, the coo of a dove, the unusual whistle of the night birds. But tonight silence surrounded Him.

There wasn't even a breeze to rustle the leaves. The garden seemed stillborn.

Then off in the distance came a low rumble. A spring storm moved down the Jordan Valley. Jesus did not see the lightning, but He heard the groan of heaven. One by one, the stars were extinguished by the fast-moving clouds. On His recent vigils in the garden, Jesus had enjoyed the light of the moon and stars, but tonight heaven seemed shut up.

"*Why?*" Jesus' heart cried out.

Disturbed by the distant thunder, Jesus rose and returned to where He had left Peter, James and John. There He found them sleeping soundly. He knew the weakness of being physically tired, but was disappointed that their professed love had not driven them to prayer. He shook Peter's shoulder to ask, "Could you men not stay awake and keep watch with me for even one hour?"

The three were embarrassed and could say nothing. Peter hung his head; John looked off into the distance.

"Keep alert," Jesus warned them. "Watch and pray or temptation will overcome you." The need to continue in prayer overwhelmed Him, and He turned to walk away. Looking back, He said to them, "Your spirit is willing, but the flesh is weak. Watch and pray."

Jesus returned once more to the spot where He had knelt and prayed, "*My Father, if it's not possible for this cup of suffering to be taken away unless I first drink it . . . then may Your will be done.*"

He knew that in the morning there would be humiliation, pain, torture and finally death by the worst form of execution possible, yet He yielded to the Father's greater plan. There was no getting around it. He would have to go through the cross to get back to His home in heaven.

"*My Father,*" Jesus continued to pray, "*My Father, why must I go through the cross?*" Each time He came to the same conclusion:

"Nevertheless, not My will, but Yours be done."

Jesus heard the sound of snoring and went again to His disciples, finding them sound asleep. "Why can't you keep your eyes open?" Jesus asked, but none of them moved.

Again, Jesus was overcome with anguish. He walked away from those whom He called "friends." Lesser men had faced execution without a whimper, but lesser men did not wrestle for the souls of mankind. Lesser men did not understand what it meant to suffer the wrath of God.

Again, collapsing under the load of grief, Jesus fell to the ground. Clutching His fists and tightening His every muscle, Jesus struggled with fear. Drops of blood beaded on His forehead, running down into His beard. Perspiration dampened His whole body as He prayed with ferocity unknown to any man before or since. His face appeared to have been bloodied by an opponent.

Satan, His adversary, gloated over the prostrate form of Jesus, certain that ultimate victory was at hand. Then an angel from heaven came to Jesus and renewed His strength, and Satan withdrew for the moment.

After a time, Jesus gathered Himself and returned to His three most trusted disciples, the three who loved Him most. They were asleep.[1]

"Anguished" is a terrible word; it is excruciating or agonizing pain in either the body or the soul. Jesus suffered acutely when He mentally faced the sufferings of the cross. His anguish began in His soul and slowly trickled throughout His being. *Lord, You anguished because of sin.*

Can almighty God anguish? A smart man can usually get out of suffering. A rich man can buy his way out of most suffering. Why did God anguish over the prospect of the cross?

Because only God knew the terrible nature of sin, while we are blinded by it. Only God knew the fierceness of His judgment, while we rationalize it away. Only God knew the torture of hell, and Jesus anguished over the punishment of hell for us.

Since Jesus anguished so much for us, how can we not give Him our service and worship? Why can we not do everything for Him?

My Time to Pray

Lord, I don't like to suffer anything physically,
And I hate any emotional or mental suffering.
Yet You went through the mental anguish of the cross,
Only hours before the physical suffering of Calvary.
Lord, thank You for Your sacrifice and courage.
Thank You for all the anguish You endured for me.
May I be willing to suffer for You
If and when persecution comes to me.
Amen.

Note
1. Adapted from Elmer Towns, *The Son* (Ventura, CA: Regal Books, 1999), pp. 265-267. See Matthew 26:36-56; Mark 14:32-52; Luke 22:40-53; John 18:1-11.

24

God Quenches

*If anyone thirsts, let him come drink of Me. When someone
believes in Me, their thirst is quenched for the ultimate satisfaction in
life, then living waters shall flow from their inner being.*
JOHN 7:37-38, *AMP*

She stood as the marriage vows were repeated. This was the happiest day of her life. She was getting the thing she wanted most in life—marriage. She dreamed of this day, planned for this day and carefully prepared for this day—a special dress, beautiful flowers and friends and family in attendance.

What about the husband? He was nothing to brag about, just an average carpenter's apprentice who promised to work hard and provide a home.

After the marriage, they lived in a small room in the back of his parents' home. The big house would be theirs when the parents died, but the parents were middle-aged and in good health. They wouldn't die anytime soon. After six months, her dreams became blurry. Marriage to the carpenter didn't make her happy, and she was getting cabin fever.

A wealthy businessman had repeatedly hired her husband to build something in his large villa. She began to dream of that home as the businessman kept adding new luxuries. The only thing the carpenter-apprentice couldn't give him was a wife, but the young man didn't realize the fat proprietor had "eyes" for his wife and was flirting with her when the carpenter was busy at his craft.

The businessman was sloppy, boorish and short-tempered with people. The young girl was blinded to his unkempt body and irritable disposition. She dreamed of the villa and believed it would make her happy.

Less than a year after her first marriage, she was divorced and remarried as a trophy wife for the businessman. His villa was the house of her dreams.

The young wife was happy with her house for only a couple of years until it dawned on her that bricks and mortar can't make one happy.

The young wife lost her enthusiasm for the villa and began taking long walks in the surrounding hills. She fell in love with the trees, brooks and nature. She now looked at the world through different eyes. God's creation enchanted her, and she spent more time outdoors. She had a small garden planted near the house with a pond, trees, flowers and some large rocks that were hauled in to make it feel like a natural pasture. But the garden didn't satisfy, so the walks in the hills became longer.

On one of her walks, she met a shepherd, and they talked of nature and God's handiwork. She began to dream of sharing her life with a soulmate. She no longer cared about a villa. She dreamed of long conversations and evenings watching the sun go down with a shepherd-lover. Her dreams of a rich villa died, and her second divorce soon followed.

However after her hasty marriage to the shepherd, she quickly found the ground too hard for sleep, and the bugs too bothersome. Sheep were dirty, and the food was not as appetizing as in the days when she thought she was in love with the shepherd.

She got tired of his dirty clothes and smelly feet. She moved into a room in town where he came to visit her every few days. Because of her fussing at him, his trips to town became less frequent.

The lonesome woman found herself spending time in the sidewalk café. She talked to all the men and fantasized about which one would make a good husband. She thought her good looks and winsome personality could catch any man she targeted.

Quickly there were two more marriages, one to the owner of the restaurant where strong drink could be purchased. She soon left him because all he wanted was someone to wait on his customers. The other was to a crotchety old man who promised her all his money if she would comfort him in his old age. She quickly tired of applying ointments, helping him walk and spoon-feeding an old man who couldn't swallow.

When she divorced the fifth husband, there was no money to pay the bills. She needed to eat, a place to sleep and to take a bath. She moved in with the town drunk. They both drank themselves to sleep at night. Now she was too drunk to dream. All of her youthful dreams faded with the realities of a harsh world.

This unnamed woman left her town of Sychar in the middle of the day to go to Jacob's Well because it was her task to fetch water for the house. Most women in Sychar went for water early in the morning and again at evening—when it was cool—where they enjoyed the company of other women and got caught up on gossip. But the town women had ostracized this lonely woman because of her lifestyle. She came alone during the middle of the day. She had been married five times and was now living with a man though not married to him. Arriving at the well, she was startled by a Jewish man sitting on a bench, who asked her a very simple question:

"Please give me something to drink."

April was usually hot, the temperature reaching 100 degrees during the last days of April. Because Jesus had already walked a long distance and was hot and thirsty, He asked for a drink of water.

The woman was surprised because Jews usually didn't have anything to do with Samaritans, especially a Samaritan woman. She responded, "Why are you asking me for a drink?"

Jesus didn't directly answer her question, but He captured her attention by saying, "If you knew who I am, and the gift of God, you would ask Me for water, and I would give you living water."

"But you don't have a rope or bucket," the woman responded. She went on to add, "The well is very deep, and there is no way for you to draw water for me."

At first the woman was concerned with the natural obstacles of getting water out of the deep well, until she realized Jesus had promised her "living water."

"You will become thirsty after drinking water from this well," Jesus explained to the woman, "but the water I will give to you will quench your thirst. You won't have to draw water again because my water will be an artesian well of water that will spring up within you, giving you eternal life."

"Please," the woman begged, "give me living water so that I will never be thirsty again. I won't have to come to this well and fetch water again."

Jesus knew the woman's heart because He was God. He knew that her sin would have to be revealed before she would seek salvation. So Jesus told her, "Go call your husband."

"I don't have a husband," the woman answered him.

"You're right." Jesus answered. "You don't have a husband now, but you have had five husbands and now you're not married to the man you're living with."

The woman came to the well to get natural water, but Jesus told her He could give her "living water" to quench her thirst for worldly satisfaction. She might have thought He was offering some magical water so that she'd never have to come to the well again. In her search for satisfaction, the woman had not found it in marriage. She had searched for the perfect mate and had not found him. Jesus said that she could find ultimate satisfaction in worshiping God (see the full story in John 4:1-42).

Just as water quenches our bodily thirst, so too fellowship with God quenches the yearnings of the soul. Jesus told the woman, "The Father in heaven seeks worship from us. The father wants us to worship Him in Spirit and truth." *Lord, I'm thirsty.*

At another time Jesus said, "If anyone thirsts, let him come to me and drink. He who believes in me, as the Scripture has said, out of his heart will flow living water" (John 7:37-38).

How can you find satisfaction? First, Jesus tells you to *come* to Him. Are you thirsty? You come to Him through prayer, simply by bowing your head and talking to Him. You come to Him by listening to His Word. You do that by reading what He tells you in the Bible. You come to Him by confessing your sins so He can restore fellowship with you. Then you enter His presence. If you are far away, why don't you take a first step to Him now? *Lord, here I come.*

The second thing that Jesus said was to *drink.* You see the cup of water and you know you're thirsty. You reach out for it with your hand and lift the cup to your lips. Tilt it so that the water flows down into your mouth. Swallow and enjoy. *Ah! Lord, Your water is good.*

My Time to Pray

Lord, I've spent time and energy seeking the wrong way
To satisfy my thirst in this world.
I've learned that things and people can't satisfy me
When I try to quench my thirst apart from You.
Lord, I realize my foolish pursuits didn't satisfy;
I repent of the silly things I did to find happiness.
I am coming to You now at this present time
To find happiness of soul in You.
Lord, I love You; thank You for loving me.
I come to drink and be satisfied with the water You give.
Amen.

25

God Smiles

May the Lord bless you, and protect you.
May the Lord smile on you and be gracious to you.
May the Lord show you His favor and give you His peace.
NUMBERS 6:24-26, *TLB*

A man and wife had been studying the *Mona Lisa* for a long time, neither one saying much. The world famous painting of Mona Lisa by Leonardo DaVinci that hangs in the Louvre in Paris, France, had been one of the special works of art they wanted to see on their trip to Europe.

"What do you admire most?" the husband asked.

"The mix of colors and shadowing," answered the wife. "I can't tell if Leonardo painted early morning or late evening."

"Why is this a world famous painting?" the husband asked.

"The woman in the painting has alluring features, although she's not especially beautiful," the wife answered. Then she added, "We can't tell much about her. There's so much mystery in the painting."

The man looked at the painting from the left, and then from the right. He wanted to see if different light on the *Mona Lisa* solved some of the mystery. Then his face lit up as if he had found the secret to Mona Lisa. "I can't tell if she's smiling or not!" Before his wife could answer, the husband continued, "I can't tell what she's smiling about."

A smile communicates many messages. The *Mona Lisa* smile could express a timid shyness or an irritating smugness. She could be saintly or regretful. Calm and confident or tentative and unsure about what she's going to do. She could be cynical or rueful. The *Mona Lisa* is world famous—not because of what we know about her smile—but because of what we don't know.

Did you know that God smiles?

Why does He smile and when does He smile? Has God ever smiled on you? Would you like Him to smile on you today?

Webster has several definitions for smile: first, "to wonder" or "to be caught by surprise." Yes, God smiles but He's never surprised because He knows all things, at all times, both actual and potential.

The second part of the definition is "to look or regard with amusement or ridicule." Again this is not the reason God smiles. God didn't create us for His amusement, nor does He ridicule us.

The third part of the definition is "to approve or express happiness."[1] This is why God smiles.

What makes God happy? When I (Elmer) approach the Father through the blood of His Son, He accepts me in grace. When I completely yield my selfish plans and projects to Him, God takes me into His care. When I attempt to serve Him with all my heart, mind and strength, saying, "Not I, but Christ," God embraces me. When I seek to know Him intimately, saying, "He is my all in all," then God smiles. *Lord, I love Your smile.*

When God smiles, I know He is happy with me. Isn't a smile one of the greatest experiences that a person can have? Greater than the pleasure of receiving any gift, greater than any reward or greater than any promotion, a smile reflects your oneness with another person. To know God personally, and to realize that He accepts me and is happy with me—because He smiles at me—is the greatest thing in life. *Lord, I look forward to Your daily smile.*

The Scripture at the beginning of this chapter is the benediction pronounced by a priest when dismissing a worshiper who has come to bring a gift or sacrifice to God. The person has supposedly come with the right attitude and has brought the right sacrifice to the right place. The priest offers the gift to God for the worshiper, and then to conclude the worship experience, he pronounces this benediction that includes, "May the LORD's face smile upon you" (Num. 6:25).

If you want God's blessing, make sure your heart has the right attitude when you approach God. Make sure you've done the right thing and approach God in the right way. *Lord, teach me how to properly approach You.*

Some don't know how to approach God, so they don't enjoy God's smile, just as a child doesn't get a parent's smile when the child is mischievous or rebellious. What about a spouse? We don't get a smile from our spouse when we knowingly do something they don't like.

We (both Charles and Elmer) like a smile from our wife; it makes life easier when she smiles. It's what marriage is all about!

What about God's smile? Isn't His smile what Christianity is all about?

My Time to Pray

Lord, when I heard that You smile,
It made me realize that You love me, and I can please You.
Lord, teach me how to reach Your heart,
And give me the ability to love You with all my heart.
Lord, I yield all of myself to You this day;
I seek You with all of my heart,
Smile on me and be gracious to me, give me Your peace.
Amen.

Note

1. *Webster's New Collegiate Dictionary* (Springfield, MA: Merriam-Webster Inc., 1976), s. v. "smile."

26

God Gets Jealous

God is jealous . . . and is furious. The LORD *will take*
vengeance on His adversaries.
NAHUM 1:2

When I (Elmer) was a freshman at Columbia Bible College, I
began to fall in love with the most beautiful girl on campus,
Ruth Forbes. But our first date was actually a planning session
for us to date other people. On our first date I planned to set up
my friend Dwayne Black to date Ruth. Ruth thought Dwayne
was handsome and successful because he was president of our
freshman class. On that date Ruth planned to set up Mary
Faith Philips to date me because I thought Mary Faith was the
smartest girl in our class.

After our date together, our plan worked. I dated Mary
Faith and Ruth dated Dwayne.

Then Ruth and I had a second date to talk about our date
the previous week. Then we had another date to talk about it
again. We became good friends and just assumed we'd go out
with each other every succeeding weekend.

When I found myself having some deep feelings for Ruth,
a fly spoiled the ointment. My best friend Art Winn asked Ruth
for a date on the same night I expected to go out with her.

Then for the first memorable time the green-eyed monster of jealousy got me. I became furiously angry at Art—my best friend—even though we had never had a disagreement for six years. I was so angry at him, I never wanted to see him again.

Only in my jealousy did I realize my deep feelings for Ruth. Then I told her, "I think I'm falling in love with you." Ruth told me she had thought about going out with Art, but would not have gone through with it. Art had instigated my jealousy, not Ruth.

Jealousy is a real emotion, whether you've felt it or not. Its potential is always present, and the green-eyed monster will arise whenever something comes between you and the thing you love.

When giving the Ten Commandments, God explained to His people that He could be jealous. He gave His people the first commandment: "Thou shalt have no other gods before me" (Exod. 20:3). Then God gave a second commandment that was an outgrowth of the first, saying, "You shall not make for yourself a carved image—any likeness of anything that is in heaven above, or that is in the earth beneath, or that is in the water under the earth; you shall not bow down to them nor serve them. For I, the LORD your God, am a jealous God" (Exod. 20:4-5).

Wow, God warned us that we could make Him jealous if we let anything get between Him and us. *Lord, I confess that You have not always been first in my life; forgive me.*

There is a twofold action that produces jealousy: first, when the object of your love turns away, and second, when the object of your love gives love to something or someone else.

God has a jealous streak and it shows itself when the people He loves turn their backs on Him and worship idols. Jealousy is the result of a broken relationship.

Is it possible for you to make God jealous? Yes! You must not have a god between you and Him. But if you turn from God to a false god, say, to the god of illicit sex, you make Him jealous. There are other gods that make Him jealous: the false god of entertainment, the demanding god of business success or the god of egotistical accomplishments. While we think these things may be good in themselves, beware that they don't slip between you and God. He is a jealous God. *Lord, I don't want to make You jealous.*

Remember, if you are a true follower of God, you have "Christ in you" (Col. 1:27). Paul gave this testimony: "For me to live is Christ" (Phil. 1:21). Christ must become first in everything; first in love, first in obedience, and first in affection.

Jealousy is the backside of love. You don't get jealous over people you don't love. You're probably not even jealous when casual friends allow other things to become more important than you. You've done the same thing to some of your casual friends. While your friends seem important in your life, your children are much more important. Will your friends get jealous over your priority to your children? Probably not! The same is true with your job; you must support yourself and your family. Your casual friends don't get jealous over that.

The deepest jealousy is felt when the one you love the most turns his/her back on you to love another. God loves everyone in the world, but He has greater love for His followers who have taken up their cross to follow Christ. Since God is perfect, He is perfect love. Also, since God is eternal, He has eternal love. Everything that is superior can be said about God's love. So when you turn your back on perfect love, His perfect jealousy sets in. *Lord, forgive me for the times I've neglected You.*

God expects you to love Him with all your heart, soul, strength and mind (see Matt. 22:37). Is it possible that even little things that get between you and God make Him jealous? Yes. Jealousy is always a possibility, and we must always strive with all our strength to put God first in our hearts. *Lord, I love You with all my heart.*

My Time to Pray

Lord, I know jealousy exists because I've felt human jealousy;
So I realize that it's only natural for You to be jealous
When I put something or someone before You.
Forgive me for being callous toward You;
Forgive me for giving You second place in my life.
Lord, I realize I've spurned Your unfailing love;
Forgive me for my spiritual stupidity.
I recommit myself to love You with all my heart,
And I place You at the center of my life.
Amen.

27

God Punishes Sin

He had looked around at them with anger,
being grieved by the hardness of their hearts.
MARK 3:5

Jesus and the disciples stood at the golden gate to Herod's Temple. It was a beautiful, warm spring day in AD 26. The Temple was crowded as people prepared for Passover, the holiest day of the year.

When they entered the Temple, however, Jesus' face fell. The disciples were worried. They had expected Jesus to show excitement coming to God's house; after all, they believed Jesus was the Messiah who would drive the Romans into the sea and set up David's throne right there in Jerusalem. The disciples expected a great announcement, spectacular miracles or some enormous divine appearance. But instead they saw Jesus' frown of disapproval.

"Why does Jesus look like He's mad?" one disciple asked another. Then they looked into the Temple and were shocked at what they saw

Jesus had expected to hear the Levitical choir singing praise psalms or see people in worshipful meditation, but instead the Temple sounded like a market bazaar. Jesus heard people bargaining over prices or shopping for the cheapest sacrifice. At a table, customers and moneychangers were arguing over the exchange rate. Children were chattering and a donkey brayed.

When Jesus could take it no longer, He climbed to a wall and shouted to the crowd, "MAKE NOT MY FATHER'S HOUSE A MARKET PLACE!"

Jumping from the wall, He turned over the tables of moneychangers, yelling at them, "OUT!" He pointed out the East Gate. "LEAVE IMMEDIATELY!"

The crowd was too shocked to reply. They watched with wonder as Jesus moved from table to table, scattering coins on the stone pavement. Children laughed with glee as they chased coins rolling in every direction.

Then Jesus twisted some ropes together to lay stripes on an ox. It bolted toward the Temple gate with its owner running to retrieve his merchandise. The crowd laughed.

The crowd didn't yell at Jesus, nor did anyone try to stop Him. The Holy Spirit froze them in terror. There was enough God-consciousness left in them to tell them they were wrong. The Father in heaven felt the same anger as His Son. God first came in the Shekinah cloud when Solomon prayed to dedicate the Temple. The inhabitants worshiped in a holy hush. But a holy hush was not present in the Temple that day; instead there was a carnival atmosphere. Then the crowd heard Jesus shout, "My Father's house is a house of prayer; you have made it a den of thieves."

The disciples didn't help Jesus turn over the moneychangers' tables, nor did they drive out any of the sacrificial animals. They were riveted by Jesus' angry explosion. Everything they had experienced of Jesus had been kind and loving. But this . . .

One disciple quoted Psalm 69 in his attempt to understand what he saw: "My devotion to your house, O God, burns in me like a fire" (John 2:17, *TEV*).

Most think God is a loving Father, but this image of an angry Jesus (found in Matthew 21:12-17, Mark 11:15-19, Luke 19:45-48 and John 20:13-16) goes against any modern perception of a smiling Jesus surrounded by children or a compassionate Jesus healing the multitude. Yes, God is love, but God is also holy, which means He's separate from anything that's sinful or rebellious. To fully understand God, you must realize God punishes sin. He does it because He is angry with our sin.

Those who think Jesus is only love and blessings have only seen one side of Him. The same is true of God the Father. Those who think of God as a kind, genteel old grandfather have only seen one side of God.

When a mother constantly tells her son to not touch a hot frying pan, and he continually reaches for it, what does she do? Does she let him touch the pan and possibly scar his hand forever? No! She spanks the hand to teach obedience and to protect her son. She doesn't spank to hurt her son, and she doesn't like to see him cry for the sake of tears.

What should God do when His children constantly disobey Him? If God looked the other way, He would deny the standards that reflect His nature. His anger at our disobedience is the other side of His love that protects us. He can let us scar ourselves forever or He can correct us with a "pat" on the hand. God's love takes over to correct and teach us.

But when we constantly disobey Him when we know better, then God's anger is seen because He must discipline us.

When you stumble, a gentle Jesus picks you up. When you ignorantly disobey God and constantly turn your back on Him, what should you expect? God says, "My son, don't be angry when the Lord punishes you. When he whips you it proves you are really his child" (Heb. 12:5-6, TLB). *Lord, I will be quick to obey You.*

Jesus was angry because the priests who taught the Scriptures should have known better. They were housekeepers of

God's house, and they let it get dirty. They knew it was wrong to sell merchandise in God's house, but they did it to make money. No wonder Jesus was angry. *Lord, may I never do anything to get You angry at me.*

Has Jesus ever been angry with you? Have you ever felt His stern rebuke? If so, repent immediately. Tell Him you're sorry. If tears don't come, maybe you have a hardened heart. Pray until God touches your heart. Then continue praying until you can touch Him.

My Time to Pray

Lord, I know You are a loving God; the Bible teaches
That You love me unconditionally.
But my sin breaks my fellowship with You,
Especially when I keep returning to my sin.
No wonder You get angry with Your rebellious children.
Lord, I am sorry for my stupid selfishness;
I repent of my dumb disobedience.
I do love You with all my heart;
Forgive me for my appetite for sin
And my neglect of Your standards of holiness.
Lord, don't be angry forever with me.
Look on my repentance with favor;
I want to always feel Your love.
Amen.

28

God Frowns

"Come back to Me, Israel," announces the LORD.
"I will frown on you no longer."
JEREMIAH 3:12, ELT

"Everyone please stay in the picture," a father pleaded with his parents and children. It was Thanksgiving Day, and he wanted to get a family portrait before everyone dove into the turkey dinner.

"I've got to go to the bathroom," a little fellow pleaded, so he took off up the stairs. A family portrait is not complete without all the little folks, so the camera had to wait.

Then a teen stepped into the family room to check on the football score, and Mother dashed into the kitchen to turn down the stove. "I'll be right back," she yelled.

When the little fellow returned, the father yelled to the teenage boy, "Come on, son!" Then he directed his irritated voice to the kitchen, "We can't take this picture without you, honey."

Finally everyone was in place, but no one seemed happy about it. "Come on, guys," the father directed his displeasure to all. "Smile."

The moment of truth arrived, so the father counted, "One, two, three . . . Frown!" Everyone laughed, because it was the opposite of what they expected. They expected the father to command "Smile." A frown is the opposite of a smile, and isn't a smile an upside-down frown?

Webster's tells us that the word "frown" comes from the Celtic *froigner*, which meant to "snort" or "show facial displeasure."[1] A frown is when the disappointment we feel on the inside is seen on our face.

We frown, but can God feel displeasure? Can God frown? Yes, God can frown because He can feel displeasure when His children disobey Him or rebel against Him.

There's a second part of the definition of "frown." It's when we wrinkle our forehead because we just can't figure things out. A wrinkled forehead is a frown. Is God ever in deep concentration because He's perplexed? No! Since God knows all things, there is never a time when God doesn't know what's going on or He can't figure things out. God is omniscient. He knows all things perfectly at all times. So when someone says God frowns, it's not because He doesn't know what's happening. He knows.

Finally there's a third part of the definition of "frown." It's when we raise an eyebrow because we are in deep thought, bewildered or can't remember. Can God forget? No, God knows all things, all the time. If He didn't, then God is not God, and that could never happen. So God doesn't frown in deep thought, searching for a thought He's forgotten. He knows.

When God frowns, it's because of His displeasure with our disobedience. Someone might ask how God can be displeased with us. Doesn't the Bible say, "The blood of Jesus Christ cleanses from all sin" (1 John 1:7)? Yes, God forgives all sins, and He cleanses our heavenly record, but there are earthly consequences to our actions. God's children may lie, steal or even kill. They shouldn't, but they do. Didn't David commit adultery and then lie to cover up the deed, finally arranging the murder of Uriah to make the problem go away? The Bible says,

"But the thing that David had done displeased the LORD" (2 Sam. 11:27). If we could have seen God's face, He would have been frowning.

God forgave David's sin, but the results messed up the kingdom. Yes, God cleansed David's record in heaven, but there was a baby in the palace that was conceived outside of marriage. There was a planned murder of the husband. When David's general was included in the plot, David's circle of sin was extended even further.

God frowned because He had gone the extra mile to give David everything. God called David to be king over Israel. Then God gave him victory over Goliath and all the other heathen armies that attacked him. God allowed him to capture Jerusalem and then gave David a luxurious palace. In the face of God's gifts, David sinned. Can we say God will frown greater if we sin in the face of God's greater gifts to us? *Lord, may I never displease You.*

The verse at the beginning of this chapter declares, "'Come back to Me, Israel,' announces the LORD. 'I will frown on you no longer'" (Jer. 3:12, *ELT*). Remember, God delivered Israel from slavery in Egypt and brought her through the Red Sea. He miraculously provided water and manna in the wilderness, and then gave the Promised Land to Israel, a land flowing with milk and honey.

But Israel turned her back on God, worshiping false idols even in the Temple. Israel lived like the nations around her and committed adultery. No wonder God frowned on Israel.

But God promises, "I will frown on you no longer." What does Israel have to do to get into God's pleasure? He says, "Return, faithless Israel." *Lord, I repent now of all my sins.*

Notice what happens when someone frowns. They usually want to scold or criticize, either with words or facial rejection. When we see a frown, it's a rebuke or blame. We're being admonished or reproached. I surely don't want God's scolding or rejection. *Lord, don't reject me; I come humbly to You, asking for forgiveness by the blood of Christ.*

My Time to Pray

Lord, I want what is promised in the Levitical benediction:
Lord, may you bless me and protect me.
Lord, may you smile on me and be gracious to me.
Lord, may You show Your favor to me, and give me peace
(see Num. 6:24-26, AMP).

Note

1. *Webster's New Collegiate Dictionary* (Springfield, MA: Merriam-Webster Inc., 1976), s.v. "frown."

29

God Cries

Jesus wept.
JOHN 11:35

On the east side of Jordan, known for its rugged terrain, the disciples huddled around the fire to keep warm. It was the winter of AD 29, and all they could think of was staying warm by the fire.

"Look . . . someone's coming." At that announcement everyone looked at the servant approaching the camp. "That's the servant of Mary and Martha . . . and he looks worried." The servant did not greet anyone but went straight to Jesus with a message.

"Lazarus is about to die; Mary and Martha want you to come immediately." The disciples looked from one worried face to another. They all realized the Jews tried to kill Jesus when He was recently in Jerusalem. Without saying anything, their body language indicated they didn't want to return to Jerusalem, and they didn't want Jesus to go there either.

Jesus waited two days. Why? Jesus knew what the disciples didn't know. Lazarus was dying at that very moment. Before the day would be over, Lazarus would be dead. Jesus didn't choose to heal Lazarus at a distance, nor did He choose to leave immediately for the metro Jerusalem area where Lazarus lived.

Several things must have gone through Jesus' mind while He waited. *The disciples are worried about dying, but I am life. The sisters are complaining because I didn't come when they beckoned me, but I control the day a person dies.*

Two days later Jesus said, "Let's go." The disciples still didn't want to go near Jerusalem. Some were afraid that Jesus might die; others feared for their own lives. Jesus was sad that His followers didn't realize who He was, nor did they believe He could protect Himself. If He could heal a leper, still a storm, feed 5,000 and do many other miracles, why couldn't they believe His ability to make good choices?

It took two days to get to the outskirts of Bethany. Martha met Jesus with a veiled criticism. "If you had been here," she told Jesus, "my brother Lazarus would not have died." Martha believed Jesus could prevent death, but she didn't believe He could raise Lazarus from the dead.

Word of Jesus' arrival reached the house where solemn Mary was mourning. She came immediately to the cemetery and said to Jesus, "If you had been here, my brother would not have died." Does that sound familiar? It's the same thing her sister had said to Jesus. It sounds like they complained to each other. Since we don't know Mary's heart, we don't know if she was trying to give Jesus a guilt trip or if this was outright criticism.

"He's been dead four days," the disciples may have said to each other. "What can Jesus do?"

When Jesus got to the grave, He saw Mary weeping, and the Jews that came with her weeping. What would you expect to happen next? Here is Jesus, the Son of God, standing in the presence of a corpse. Two sisters weeping. The crowd weeping. The disciples who might not have believed He could resurrect the corpse. All rejected Jesus in one way or another; they wouldn't recognize or believe Him.

And what did Jesus do? He cried!

Here was a grown man crying. Most men don't like to cry; it shows their tender side, or as they think, their weak side. Men want people to think they are strong and can endure any physical or emotional pain. Men want people to think they can overcome barriers or problems. So men don't cry.

But Jesus wept.

Why did Jesus shed tears? As this story told in John 11:1-44 indicates, it is because He wanted people to believe in Him, but they didn't. Jesus cried because of the people's unbelief in His power to raise the dead. He was the only one there who could do something about the crisis, but no one believed He could do what He was going to do.

What makes God cry? Unbelief. When an individual refuses to believe in God, God is broken-hearted.

Why is God broken-hearted?

Because Christ died for their sins and they refuse to accept the benefits of His sacrifice.

Because they will go to hell for all eternity where there is no escape, and there is no end.

Because God has done all He can do to save them.

Because they will simply not believe in Him.

What makes you cry? Sometimes it's physical pain, like a broken bone or a headache. Sometimes it's because people have had something stolen from them, like a possession, money or something valuable. Sometimes it's disappointment, whether you've disappointed yourself or someone else has disappointed you. We cry when we hurt with physical or emotional pain.

But what hurts God?

Unbelief hurts God because it's the one thing God doesn't expect of His followers. He wants us to trust in Him with all our hearts (see Prov. 3:5). Call it trust, reliance, following or surrender—when we believe in God, we know that He exists, and we know He rewards those who diligently seek Him (see Heb. 11:6). *Lord, may I never doubt You so that I may never make You weep.*

My Time to Pray

Lord, there have been times I've doubted You;
Forgive me for breaking Your heart.
There have been times when I've trusted myself,
More than trusting You—forgive me.
Lord, thank You for Your never-ending love for me.
May I never take Your love lightly.
May I never make You weep.
Amen.

God Has Strength
and Beauty

When Abram was ninety-nine years old, the Lord appeared to Abram and said to him, "I am Almighty God; walk before Me and be blameless."
GENESIS 17:1

He who dwells in the secret place of the Most High shall abide under the shadow of the Almighty.
PSALM 91:1

The title "Almighty" suggests God satisfies and gives us strength. His almighty, loving care makes us strong:

I (Elmer) knew my mother loved me. She showed it in many ways, but none greater than the meals she cooked for me. My mother loved to cook. She did it intuitively, putting together an exotic cake, crab soufflé or a simple egg omelet by feel. As I like to say, she cooked from her heart.

My mother didn't have a cookbook that I remember, nor did she have measuring spoons or cups. She'd pour in milk till it felt right, and then added the measured ingredients by estimation: salt, chives or nutmeg. She never followed an exact memorized recipe the same way twice, but all her meals were magnificent, if not perfect.

She could create grand feasts on an outdated electric range or a wood-burning stove when we stayed at my grandpa's house. Heat was heat.

Her vegetables came out of her garden, grown without man-made fertilizer, but enriched with animal fertilizer. Mother also had her own homemade enriched organic mulch. She turned our backyard that looked like a sandy beach into rich loam to produce a large harvest that enriched all our neighbors with all the vegetables they needed. Providing good food was Mother's passion.

We always had three or four vegetables with each meal, and plenty of eggs from our chickens. To make sure I became strong and healthy, I never once had a carbonated drink with a meal, only milk or water.

Mother read the vitamin books and made sure we had a proper mixture of green and yellow vegetables. We had a perfect balance of above-ground leafy vegetables and below-ground roots. Also we had a proper mixture of cooked and fresh vegetables.

Mother had a special interest in making sure I got the right vegetables to make me strong, yet she also wanted me to enjoy eating them. My favorite was small sugar peas that came from plain field peas. She'd pick the smallest for me, sear them quickly in a sizzling frying pan with a little vegetable oil and dish them piping hot straight to my plate—half raw or half cooked.

After crafting her culinary masterpieces, she would sit to enjoy watching me eat. Her greatest joy was her healthy, happy children.

God is a lot like my mother. Though I guess the analogy should be reversed: my mother was a lot like God, especially the almighty God. While we immediately think the word "almighty" denotes strength, that's not its primary meaning. It means a sensitive God who gives nourishment and pleasure to His children because He cares for them. He nourishes them to make them strong. The word "almighty" (*El Shaddai*) comes from the word "breast." When we think of a woman, it reminds us of nourishment for babies to make them strong. When applied to the chest of a man, it symbolizes his strength.

Do you realize God can be tender and strong at the same time? It's almost an oxymoron, like using tough blue denim to make lace. But what seems impossible with men is possible with God. He is strength and beauty.

The first time the name *El Shaddai* (Almighty) occurs in Scripture, God comes to 99-year-old Abraham to tell him he'll have a son. That birth was something God promised over 25 years earlier. Now Abraham is too old to father a son. It's against the laws of nature for a 99-year-old man to have children, especially when he's married to an 89-year-old wife.

God is offering His strength to elderly Abraham, and this offer is a beautiful picture. The strength is God's life-giving miracle that Abraham will have a son. God's beauty demonstrates to the world that God keeps His promises.

But the scene also demonstrates the tenderness of God. Earlier Abraham doubted God's promise, so old Abraham proposed Eliezer as an heir. Abraham prayed, "O Sovereign Lord, what can you give me since I remain childless and the one who will inherit my estate is Eliezer of Damascus?" (Gen. 15:2). God answered abruptly, "This one shall not be your heir" (Gen. 15:4).

Then apparently Abraham felt that God helps those who help themselves, so he fathered a son by a slave-wife, Hagar. Because fellow leaders of Bedouin tribes had children by a concubine, this son—Ishmael—became the delight of Abraham's old age. Abraham probably thought Ishmael, whose mother was not Sarah, would be the one through whom Messiah would come.

For 13 years Abraham raised his son Ishmael, probably teaching him to hunt, fish and ride a horse. Abraham poured his hopes into Ishmael, but Ishmael was not God's plan.

So God came tenderly to 99-year-old Abraham to tell him he would be a father, and his wife Sarah would be a mother. What would be your reaction? Abraham laughed. "Then Abraham fell on his face and laughed, and said in his heart, 'Shall a child be born to a man who is one hundred years old? And shall Sarah, who is ninety years old, bear a child?'" (Gen. 17:17).

God wanted to do something special for Abraham, so God gave His friend Abraham the one thing that only God can give—life. Because God is the source of life, He gave life to Abraham. *Lord, thank You for the gift of eternal life.*

My mother was married to an alcoholic husband, and seldom had any extra money for the luxuries of life. So what did my mother give her son? She gave me her very best talents: cooking and gardening vegetables. Tenderly she gave me the staff of life.

Would you like the Almighty to strengthen you for life's pressures or to overcome insurmountable barriers? Then look again at the Scriptures: "He who dwells in the secret place of the Most High shall abide under the shadow of the Almighty" (Ps. 91:1).

Notice two things you must do. First you must assume an attitude of abiding in God's care. Aren't we instructed, "If you abide in Me, and My words abide in you . . ." (John 15:7)? To abide means to rest or settle down in the Lord. So stop fighting Him. Reflect on His heart. *Lord, here I come to rest in You.*

The second thing you must do is to be in the shadow of the Almighty. We have to get close to a person—real close—to get their shadow to cover us. Just as a mother doesn't want her little toddler out of her shadow, so too we must snuggle up to the Almighty if we expect Him to strengthen and nourish us for our task in life.

My Time to Pray

Lord, let me stand close to You so that
Everyone will know I identify with You.
When I'm standing next to You,
I'll learn how to live for You.
Lord, I want to abide in Your shadow
So I can receive Your nourishment to grow strong.
When You deal with me tenderly,
That is a beautiful thing.
Amen.

31

God Can Be Pleased

But without faith it is impossible to please Him,
for he who comes to God must believe that He is, and that
He is a rewarder of those who diligently seek Him.
HEBREWS 11:6

Napoleon's French army had invaded a remote island in the Mediterranean Sea. Resistance was fierce and there was a large loss of life on both sides. Finally, the island was secure and all resistance was wiped out.

According to Napoleon's custom, a large banquet was thrown for his officers to reward those with outstanding accomplishments in battle. Each officer nominated his troops for bravery or great accomplishments, but of course, Napoleon himself decided who would get rewards.

After the rewards were handed out, everyone settled into eating, drinking and merriment. It was then that a young lieutenant approached Napoleon, snapped to attention and saluted.

"What do you want?" Napoleon returned the salute.

The room got deathly silent. All the other officers were appalled that a lowly lieutenant would approach the most successful general in all of Europe. For such insolence, other lowly officers had been demoted or confined to their quarters. Silence imprisoned the room.

"What do you want?" Napoleon repeated his question.

"Sir," the lieutenant replied, standing motionless, "give me this island. It's my boyhood home!"

The room of officers was aghast. Their incredulous unbelief publicly exploded.

Quickly, Napoleon asked for paper, turned his back to the room and scribbled something. Smiling, the general handed the young lieutenant the paper, and then announced to the room, "The island is his; that's a title deed."

Now the officers were even more bewildered. Dumbfounded, they looked to one another for an answer. They all wanted to ask the same question, "Why?" The second in command turned to Napoleon to ask, "We have lost many loyal French soldiers in the battle for this island. Why would you capture it to give it to a lowly lieutenant?"

Napoleon answered, "He honored me with the magnitude of his request."

Napoleon could have had any land he desired, and his army could have captured any that defied him. Napoleon realized that the young lieutenant had paid him the greatest compliment of all by realizing he had the military power to capture anything he desired and the political power to give it away. The young lieutenant realized Napoleon could do anything he wanted without asking anyone, and that pleased Napoleon.

If you want to please God, you must have as much faith in your heavenly Father as the young lieutenant had in Napoleon, and more so.

You please God when you totally believe that God exists. The old *King James* translation of Hebrews 11:6 said you please God when you come to the place in life where you realize that "God is."

You please God when you know that God is eternal, and you are here for just a short time. You also bring Him joy when you acknowledge He is creator of everything and gave His life so you could be saved and live for His purpose. *Lord, I know You exist, but sometimes I don't act like You're here. Forgive me!*

Faith may be the greatest of all the qualities you possess. Oh yes, faith, hope and love remain, and Paul said the greatest was love (see 1 Cor. 13:13). Paul meant love was the greatest in influencing others. But your faith is the greatest all-time power because by faith you can influence God; hope and love only influence other people.

A lot of people have asked God for something big, but didn't really believe God would give it to them. Those people didn't have faith. Some ask for really big things—like millions of dollars or for faith healing, or for some other huge request. But did they ask according to the rules of the kingdom? Can you say you have faith in God if you ask contrary to His rules? The same goes for those who ask ignorantly.

You please God when you ask according to the way He instructed you. But if you have a shallow understanding of God, you demonstrate that you lack attention to know Him and His ways. God rewards according to your faith, not your audacity.

Jesus explained this principle to us when He said, "Have faith in God" (Mark 11:22). Just recognize God, do what He says and you will please God. And when God is pleased, we can boldly ask for big things, even moving mountains. "For assuredly, I say to you, whoever says to this mountain, 'Be removed and be cast into the sea,' and does not doubt in his heart, but believes that those things he says will be done, he will have whatever he says. Therefore I say to you, whatever things you ask when you pray, believe that you receive them, and you will have them" (Mark 11:23-24).

Saying what you want is not the key to moving the mountains in your life. *Naming* it is not the key to *claiming* it. It's your faith that pleases God so that He rewards you.

If there is a secret to faith, it's wrapped up in one word—*relationship*. You think you know your spouse when you stand before a preacher to get married, but it's really only just the beginning of a relationship. You'll know each other much more intimately after 50 years of marriage. In the same way, after living with God for 50 years, you will know God more intimately and be able to better please Him. If you believe God exists and is worthy of one or two hours of time a day, you will please Him. And the more you know Him, the better your faith can honor God with the magnitude of your request. That faith will move mountains as God rewards you.

Reflect on the heart of God. Does your faith please Him daily or do you pretty much live your life to please yourself?

My Time to Pray

Lord, forgive me for spending so little time with You,
Forgive me for knowing so little about You;
I'm sorry I've not learned how to fully obey You.
Lord, I want to move mountains that block my life,
And I want my prayers answered,
But it's my lack of faith that hinders me.
Lord, I will go deep in Scripture to learn how You answer;
I will learn to know You and fellowship with You
So You will reward my faith for the magnitude of my requests.
Amen.

32

God Collects Tears in a Bottle

Put my tears into Your bottle; are they not in Your book?
PSALM 56:8

I (Elmer) use to keep things in old quart milk bottles. My early bottles were round, but later someone found out they could store more of them together if they were square. So my later milk bottles were square.

I kept pennies in my milk bottle, but I never filled it up. When you're poor, money burns a hole in your pocket, so I'd spend my pennies long before the bottle was filled.

I used to play marbles and kept my marbles in a milk bottle, watching them sparkle in the rays of the sun. Do you remember knuckles down or your favorite shooter?

Why did I keep things in a milk bottle? Because I was a collector, and when my things were in a bottle—not a box—I could easily count to see how much I had collected.

Also, when you are poor, you value yourself by how much you collect. Let's just say I got some self-identity from collecting things. I'd say to my buddies, "Look how many marbles I've got." Then we'd compare collections. It was important not to be embarrassed by someone's much larger collection.

"Mine's shinier than yours," I probably said on occasion. I loved to put my steely marble on top of my collection. It actually was a chrome-plated ball bearing. I liked it because it glistened, but if the truth were known, I liked it because it was heavier and could knock more marbles out of the circle than a plain glass marble.

Do you think God is a collector? What things would God want to collect? Maybe God collects things for the same reason that we do. Now God would not have the same selfish motivation as we humans. But the opposite might be true; we might have pure motivation we get from God.

The opening verse to this study from Psalm 56 tells us that God has a bottle in heaven where He collects the tears of His followers. Is it an actual bottle or is it a metaphorical bottle that reflects His concern for us? In the Old Testament a bottle probably referred to a leather water skin; later in the New Testament, bottles were more likely to be glass. Do you think God has an actual bottle? How big is it?

God's bottle that is mentioned in this passage tells of the fear of David when captured by the Philistines in Gad. David had been running from Saul, who tried to kill him, when his life-long enemies the Philistines got him. Notice the anguish of David's prayers: "Man would swallow me up," (Ps. 56:1) moaned David. He complained to God, "My enemies would hound me all day" (Ps. 56:2). David told God, "[my enemies] twist my words" (Ps. 56:5). Therefore, in deep anguish and tears, David prayed to God for Him to "put my tears into Your bottle" (Ps. 56:8).

Did you notice it was called "Your bottle"? God has His own bottle. He doesn't need our bottle or to borrow one from someone else. God already has His bottle, so He didn't need to create one or to use human ingenuity to make one. God has His own private bottle to hold our tears. *God, do You have any of my tears in Your bottle?*

I kept things precious to me in my bottle. What is precious to God that He would keep in His bottle? Surely not the money we give to Him in the church offering plate, or the receipts for spending money on God's causes. Surely God does not keep our blue ribbons or first place trophies surrounding His bottle. God has tears in His bottle because they mean very much to Him.

Why our tears? Because our tears represent our most honest sincerity. We cry when we hurt the most. And when we pray from our deepest wounds and hurts, we pray best.

Also, we cry when we've lost all pride and self-image. When we don't care what people think of us, we hold back nothing. Tears make us genuine. *Lord, I will pray sincerely.*

God wants to keep things that are genuine. Don't art dealers want the genuine painting for their collection? They don't want a copy or a forgery. The same is true with God. He wants to remember the times in our life when we were more honest than any other time.

David was being completely honest with the Lord in this way when he penned the words to Psalm 56. God had anointed him king over Israel, and young David knew it. David had killed Goliath when Saul wouldn't go to battle. Then Saul became jealous of David and tried to kill him. The enemies of God—the Philistines—probably hadn't forgotten that David killed Goliath, their champion. Now the Philistines had David in their grasp. No wonder David was scared. He was probably more scared than when he faced Goliath. He was probably more scared than any time in his life. So David prayed honestly, sincerely and with genuine faith—so genuine that God wanted to collect His tears in a bottle.

In addition to storing David's tears in the bottle, Psalm 56:8 also tells us that God had a book. It could have been a book where God kept a record of what went into the bottle.

God wrote down when David cried, where David cried and why David cried.

For all I know, God's book could have included a ranking of all the tears of David that were in God's bottle. Let's see now, on a scale of 1 to 10, the time David prayed when captured by the Philistines could have been a 10—all other tears were a 9 or below.

I don't think so. God probably doesn't rank our tears in a book. But there is a book of works that will be opened in the future judgment (see Rev. 20:12-15). God knows the sincerity of every prayer we've ever prayed, and every work we've ever done. He'll reward us accordingly.

As I wrote this chapter, I wondered if I've had any prayers sincere enough to be recorded in God's book. But more importantly, do I have any tears in His bottle?

It's all right to weep, because Jesus wept (see chapter 29), and it's all right to laugh, because Jesus laughed (see chapter 18). The Bible teaches, "A time to weep and a time to laugh" (Eccles. 3:4).

So weep in prayer for your unsaved relatives and friends to be saved. Be one "Who continually goes forth weeping, bearing seed for sowing, shall doubtless come again with rejoicing, bringing his sheaves with him" (Ps. 126:6).

Also, there is a time to weep when we fully face our sins in the presence of the Lord Jesus Christ. A fallen woman came behind Jesus, "And stood at His feet behind Him weeping" (Luke 7:32). What good did her tears do? Jesus said, "Her sins, which are many, are forgiven; for she loved much" (Luke 7:47). *Lord, my sins are many; forgive me.*

So if you've been weeping today, remember that your tears are precious to Jesus. They are remembered in a bottle. But look beyond your tears, for "weeping may endure for a night, but joy comes in the morning" (Ps. 30:5).

My Time to Pray

Lord, You know all things about me,
And everything else in the universe.
Thank You for loving me and accepting me,
In spite of all my weaknesses and failures.
Lord, I trust Your wisdom and knowledge.
Thank You for creating a plan for my life.
I will trust You and seek to follow You daily.
Amen.

God Has No Tomorrows

*From the tribe of Issachar there were 200 leaders of the tribe
with their relatives—all men who understood the temper of the
times and knew the best course for Israel to take.*
1 CHRONICLES 12:32

*"I am the Alpha and the Omega, the Beginning and the End," says the
Lord, "who is and who was and who is to come, the Almighty."*
REVELATION 1:8

Two pilots were flying a large airliner cross-country. The co-
pilot asked the senior pilot why he always flew nearly 50
miles out of the way over a little town in Kansas on their
cross-country flights. The senior pilot replied, "I was raised in
that little town, and I always look for the only river in the area
on the south of the city."

"Why is that?" the co-pilot asked, knowing there was a
story there.

"I used to fish on the bank of that river and lay in the grass
to dream of what I'd do when I grew up. I'd always dream of flying a plane. I figured when I got to be a pilot, I'd be the happiest
in life. I never really thought I'd ever get out of that little town."

Within a few minutes the plane approached the little town, and the pilot dipped his wings in salute to the river he had just described.

"Why'd you do that?" the co-pilot absentmindedly asked.

The pilot wistfully answered, "I thought I'd be ultimately happy when I got out of that town and got to be a pilot, but I'm not." The senior pilot poured out his problems with his kids, overspent credit cards, drinking addiction and suspected infidelity of his wife. Then he looked back once more and said, "I didn't realize how happy I was lying in the grass by that river until I left it."

Do you realize that today is the most important day in your life? Today is the tomorrow you dreamed of yesterday.

If you're not happy *now*, you won't be happy tomorrow because if you don't learn to live *now* and get the most out of *now*, you will never enjoy tomorrow.

When you reflect on the heart of God, you'll realize how urgent *today* is. God has given you the gift of time. He didn't give you the eighteenth century; He gave you *now*, so you have to use what the Lord gave you today. There's a reason why you are the child of your parents and not the reverse. Find out what God wants you to do today, and do it now.

For instance, you can learn how to live *now* when you know the benefits of yesterday. Yesterday had power and is the foundation of today. It was a school to prepare you to live today. If you didn't learn yesterday's lessons yesterday, then determine to learn them today. That way, today will be the school that will prepare you for tomorrow. Then tomorrow will be the *TODAY* that you spent learning lessons from yesterday. *Lord, let me learn from yesterday for a better today*.

Understand the power of tomorrow. Your dreams will be realized in your tomorrows, and those dreams will give energy to your life today. Dreams will drive you to work harder to accomplish them. Dreams will discipline you to sacrifice to obtain them. Dreams have the power to make you learn from yesterday so you can prepare for tomorrow. *Lord, let my dreams motivate me to prepare for tomorrow.*

Finally, learn the urgency factor of today. Why? Because while it is important to dream and plan for the future, it is also important to live in today. Live one day at a time and don't get overly anxious about what the future holds (see Matt. 6:34). When tomorrow comes, it won't be tomorrow—it will be today. You can only live one day at a time, and that day is today. *Lord, I will live now for You. Help me get everything possible out of now.*

Let's think about the sons of Issachar described in the opening verse from 1 Chronicles. They knew the times in which they lived. Notice the verse doesn't describe their past or their future, nor did it say they understood their past or their future. The fact that they knew their present times meant they learned from the school of yesterday and the dreams of tomorrow motivated their today. "They knew the times." *Lord, help me see my world through Your eyes, and help me know today.*

You can't know everything. There's no Ph.D. in history that knows all about the many yesterdays that have ever existed. Only God knows all about yesterday because He was there. Learn from Him so you'll be prepared to live today.

You can't know everything about the future. You'll never live in the tomorrow of the future. You'll only live a succession of todays. But God is already living at the day of your death. He knows when it'll happen, where it'll happen and how it'll happen. Since there is no yesterday or tomorrow for God, let Him prepare you to live today, so you'll be prepared when it comes time to die. *Lord, I commit my death to You.*

The sons of Issachar not only knew the times, but they also knew what Israel ought to do. That suggests two or three things they knew. They knew the Scriptures where God predicted the future of Israel and how Israel should be living for God. They also knew the person of God and how He related to His people. Finally, they knew what was right and what Israel had to do to get right with God and to live for God. *Lord, may I know the times as did the sons of Issachar, and may I do right.*

There is coming a day when there'll be no more time. It'll be eternal day, an eternal *NOW*. In that future day, there will be no more tomorrows to motivate you to action and self-improvement. There will be no more night. Then you'll be like the sons of Issachar; you'll know the times, and you'll know what to do.

Another thing about our future day in heaven is that there will be no yesterdays to teach us how to live. We'll know all we are supposed to know, and we'll do all we are supposed to do. There'll be no regrets in heaven over our failures of yesterday. There'll be "no more crying" (Rev. 21:4) and no memory to take away our joy. We shall be perfect like Him when we see His face (see 1 John 3:2; Rev. 22:4).

My Time to Pray

Lord, I've had a lot of failures in my yesterdays,
Forgive me for each and every one.
Lord, my tomorrows are not much better;
I've failed to accomplish much because of my past.
Lord, I didn't take care of all my todays;
Forgive me of all my failures and sins,
Those that involved my yesterdays, tomorrows and todays.
Lord, I look forward to the eternal day;
Maybe it will come tomorrow,
Then I'll live perfectly with You.
But, if it doesn't come for a long time,
I'll live for You today.
Amen.

God Is Love

For God so loved the world that He gave His only begotten Son, that whoever believes in Him should not perish but have everlasting life.
JOHN 3:16

Love is perhaps the most popular attribute of God. When children are asked to describe God, they eventually say "love." But love is not just what God shows to a person, or the compassion He expresses for a person; God is the source of love. God is love. "He who does not love does not know God, for God is love; and we have known and believed the love that God has for us. God is love, and he who abides in love abides in God, and God in Him" (1 John 4:8,16).

To say God is love makes Christianity unique among the religions of the world. Many of the gods of the heathen religion are angry; some are even hateful beings. Those who worship idols think their god punishes them, and they blame their god for every bad thing that happens to them. That's why the heathen gods need constant appeasing.

But the God of Christianity is different. He doesn't do bad things to people, but He tells us in the Bible why bad things happen. He reminds us that we live in a fallen world where germs and bacteria spread disease, where hateful people do hateful things, where accidents harm us, where things break down, where rust and weeds eventually take over, and where our aging bodies weaken us. We are born into this world with no knowledge so that we must learn everything we need to know to protect ourselves, advance ourselves and provide for our life, liberty and pursuit of happiness.

We also live in a world in which people die. A little boy, standing behind the right shoulder of his dad, who was driving the family station wagon, once asked, "Does everyone have to die?"

"Yes," the father wistfully answered.

"Even if they get lucky?" the little boy chirped.

"Yes," was all that the father had to say.

Death is an enigma that chokes the life out of every person. We all know we will die. It is a pressing question that each of us must face. In fact, this question was asked in the oldest book written in the Bible: "If a man dies, shall he live again?" (Job 14:14).

God had to punish Adam and Eve because of their disobedience in the garden. If you were in the eternal theatre watching the events of the Garden of Eden unfold before your eyes, you might have asked, "Will God kill them?" Didn't God promise death if they disobeyed Him, saying, "In the day you eat, you shall die"?

Look with me at the final act in God's theatre of salvation. God didn't kill them, but someone had to die. Jesus stepped away from the throne of God to say, "I'll go to earth, to die in their place." Jesus didn't just die for Adam and Eve; He said, "I'll die for all mankind."

You might ask from your theatre seat, "Why would Jesus do that, and why would the Father let Him do that?"

"Because of love," God would answer you.

"What is love?" you ask.

"Love is giving yourself to the one you love."

The love of Jesus is described like a relationship to a friend. "Greater love has no one than this, than to lay down one's life for his friends" (John 15:13). When you try to find the greatest expression of love, it's when you give yourself for others.

Later John said, "Here is where you understand the love of God for us: it's when Jesus laid down His life for us" (1 John 3:16, *ELT*).

Then finally John said, "Here is love . . . God loved us and sent His Son to satisfy the debt we owe to Him" (1 John 4:10, *ELT*).

The greatest declaration of love is John 3:16: "For God so loved the world that He gave His only begotten Son, that whoever believes in Him should not perish but have everlasting life."

It may be possible for some people to give possessions, money or time without loving the person to whom they give, but it's impossible to totally love without giving yourself totally.

Love is the opposite of selfishness. As a matter of fact, love is perfect unselfishness. Love gives itself completely to the one it loves.

Only the strong can love because they must have strength to reach out of themselves to another. They do that in spite of what they want or need. God, who is the source of all strength, can give Himself to us because He is the source of all love. He can give Himself and never empty Himself. He can never come to the end of His love. Why?

God is perfect love, the source of love and the expression of love. He is "the God of love" (2 Cor. 13:11) and has all "the love of God" (2 Cor. 13:14).

In the *King James Version*, the love chapter of the Bible, 1 Corinthians 13, translates the word "love" as *charity*, such as: "Charity suffereth long, and is kind; charity envieth not; charity vaunteth not itself, is not puffed up . . . Charity never faileth"

(1 Cor. 13:4,8, *KJV*). Some modern readers criticize the Bible for using the out-of-date term *charity*. Yet look at why *charity* is used to get a deeper meaning of love. *Charity* meant giving time and money to a worthy cause, such as a church, the Red Cross or some other non-profit charity. Therefore those who originally wrote the *King James Bible* saw love as giving oneself to those who were thought worthy. That's love.

But God's love is far greater. "For scarcely for a righteous man will one die; yet perhaps for a good man someone would even dare to die. But God demonstrates His own love toward us, in that while we were still sinners, Christ died for us" (Rom. 5:7-8).

My Time to Pray

Lord, thank You for Your constant love to me;
Even when I sin against You,
You always forgive me and love me.
Thank You for looking after me in love,
Even when I forget to think of You.
You always love me and protect me.
Lord, thank You for Your constant love and
Continuing grace;
You love me, forgive me, and guide me;
I'm in Your constant loving care.
Amen.

John 3:16
The Greatest Verse in the Bible

For God—greatest *being*
So—greatest *degree*
Loved—greatest *affection*
The World—greatest *object of love*
That He gave—greatest *act*
His only—greatest *treasure*
Begotten—greatest *relationship*
Son—greatest *gift*
That whosoever—greatest *company*
Believeth—greatest *trust*
In Him—greatest *object of faith*
Should not perish—greatest *deliverance*
But have—greatest *assurance*
Everlasting—greatest *promise*
Life—greatest *blessing*

5

God Is Holy

The high and lofty One who inhabits eternity, whose name is Holy.
ISAIAH 57:17

"You shall be holy, for I the LORD God am holy."
LEVITICUS 19:2

If the first description of God that usually comes to our mind is His love, then second is most likely His holiness. Maybe it's because we sing "Holy, holy, holy . . ." offering praise to God for His holiness. But do we know what we mean when we call God holy?

Holiness means "to separate" or "to cut off." To be holy means to be separate from anything that is evil. It has a dual meaning: to be separate from sin and to be separated out for use by God. Stop and ask yourself, *Am I holy?* If you are honest, you will answer no. "If we claim to be sinless, we are self-deceived" (1 John 1:8, *NEB*). If any of us think we are perfect or good enough to go to heaven, we don't know God's standard. "There is none righteous, no not one" (Rom. 3:10).

What about just one sin? What if we just slip once in a while? "If we say we have never committed one sin, we make God a liar" (1 John 1:10, *AMP*).

So what's our answer to our sin? When we become a Christian, God forgives all our sin (see John 1:29), and He also declares that we are perfect or righteous in God's sight. This means we are justified in God's presence in heaven. "Being justified by faith, we have peace with God, through our Lord Jesus Christ" (Rom. 5:1). Some have tried to explain justification with the phrase "Just as if I've never sinned."

When Jesus took our sin on the cross, He gave us His perfection. So now I have positive holiness. I have the record of Jesus' perfect life transferred to my account (see 2 Cor. 5:21).

What do you mean when you pray the Lord's Prayer and say, "Hallowed be thy name . . . on earth as it is in heaven" (Matt. 6:9-10)? The word "hallowed" means holy, so you are praying for God's holiness to rule on this earth, just as it rules heaven. But this earth is a big place, so you should focus your prayer on the place you live. "Holy be your name in my life where I'm living on earth today." *Lord, be holy in my life today.*

The holiness of God is both active and passive. It is passive in that God is holy without doing or saying anything holy. He is holy because God is perfect in all He is and does, and His holiness is the perfection of His moral nature. The angels in heaven cry, "Holy, holy, holy, Lord God Almighty, who was and is, and is to come" (Rev. 4:8).

God is also actively holy. Everything He does is holy, meaning His actions are without sin. He cannot lie (see Titus 1:2) and He always speaks the truth (see John 17:17). He cannot be tempted with sin (see Jas. 1:13), and holiness is the primary motivation of all He does.

God did not make Himself holy because if He did that, then holiness is something He decided to do. It means God was not holy at one time, and He became something different from what He was. But God cannot change. God is eternal, and He's always been holy.

Most of us have a difficult time understanding the nature of holiness. It's something the human mind struggles to understand. A. W. Tozer suggests, "We cannot grasp the true meaning of divine holiness . . . it stands apart, unique, unapproachable, incomprehensible, and unattainable. The natural man is blind to it."[1]

So what can we do? David said, "If I regard iniquity in my heart, the Lord will not hear me" (Ps. 66:18). So we must confess any sin in our life (see 1 John 1:9), and constantly walk in fellowship with Christ. For the Bible says, "If we walk in the light, as He is in the light . . . the blood of Jesus Christ God's Son cleanses us from all sin" (1 John 1:7). Then we must constantly keep ourselves from any future sin (see 1 Cor. 11:30-32).

God is too holy to look on sin. That's why He turned His back on Jesus on the cross. The cross is when Jesus became sin for us. Therefore, Jesus cried out, "My God, My God why have You forsaken me" (Matt. 27:46). *Lord, thank You for becoming my sin.*

My Time to Pray

Lord, I cry "Holy, holy, holy" because You are holy.
I bow to worship in Your presence,
Knowing You are pure and without sin.
Lord, forgive my sin by the blood of Jesus Christ,
Who gave His life to die for me.
I confess my sin and repent of every known sin.
Clothe me in the righteousness of Jesus Christ.
Lord, I will worship You in Your perfection and holiness.
Accept my praise that I bring in the name of Jesus.
Amen.

Note
1. Elmer Towns, *Theology for Today* (Ft. Worth, TX: Harcourt and Brace, 1999), p. 112, #34.

36

God Is Good

So Jesus said to him, "Why do you call Me good?
No one is good but One, that is, God.
LUKE 18:19

Cameron is my (Elmer's) four-year-old great-grandson who volunteered to pray the family table blessing last Sunday. Every Sunday, I invite to lunch any of my two daughters, 10 grand-children and three great-grandchildren who are able to attend because I want to create positive memories among my family members. Sometimes it costs almost $300, but the rewards are priceless. Last Sunday, Cameron prayed in a loud voice for all to hear:

> *God is great*
> *God is good,*
> *Let us thank Him for our food,*
> *By His hand*
> *We are fed,*
> *Let us thank Him for our daily bread.*
> *Amen.*

After the prayer I congratulated him on doing a great job, and asked, "Do you really think God is good?"

"He's given me this meal, hasn't He?"

Great wisdom from a little mind! And here I had forgotten all my theology—I thought I had provided the Sunday meal.

In a broad sense, the goodness of God includes all the positive things God is and has done for us.

When the rich young ruler came to question Jesus about salvation, he asked, "Good Master, what shall I do to inherit eternal life?" (Luke 18:18). Isn't it an interesting fact that a rich man was worried about his inheritance after this life? Jesus answered him, "There is none good but one, that is, God" (Luke 18:19, *KJV*). Yes, God is good. He is not an angry God, such as is found in heathen religions. God is good in His nature, and He does good things to the race He created, specifically to His unique children.

Moses told Israel, "He [God] will do you good" (Deut. 30:5). A good God created the world and "saw that it was good" (Gen. 1:25). And a good God said, "It is not good that man should dwell alone" (Gen. 2:18), so He created Eve. Jesus calls Himself, "the good shepherd" (John 10:11). Jesus said some were "good seed" (Matt. 13:24), and He said to the Pharisees, "Many good works I have showed you" (John 10:32).

God's goodness is seen in many of His attributes and, in a greater sense, these are part of His goodness. One of these attributes, His *mercy,* represents His goodness to those in distress or misery.

When David sinned with Bathsheba, God convicted David so greatly that he thought he would go to hell (see Ps. 51). David prayed, "Have mercy upon me, O God, according to thy lovingkindness: according to the multitude of thy tender mercies, blot out my transgressions" (Ps. 51:1, *KJV*).

The Publican prayed fervently in the Temple and "would not lift up so much as his eyes unto heaven, but beat his breast saying, 'God be merciful to me a sinner'" (Luke 18:13).

Mercy flows from God who is its source. "The mercy of the Lord is from everlasting to everlasting, upon them that fear him" (Ps. 103:17).

Mercy is available to a whole range of individuals. The Bible speaks of God's mercy to His Church (see 2 Cor. 1:3), to believers (see Heb. 4:16), to Israel (see Isa. 54:7), and His mercy to those who are called (see Rom. 9:15,18). God's mercy provides truth to us that God is indeed good.

The *grace* of God is another expression of the goodness of God. God expresses His grace to the ill-deserving and to those who deserve His punishment. The grace of God is the opposite of the justice of God. In grace, God gives to people the exact opposite of what they deserve.

They deserve condemnation, but God gives them Christ.
They deserve hell, but God gives them heaven.
They deserve death, but God gives them life.
They deserve alienation, but God gives them Himself.

Grace also is unmerited favor. There was nothing in us that deserved God's goodness. "Even when we were dead in trespasses, [God] made us alive together with Christ (by grace you have been saved)" (Eph. 2:5).

In the goodness of God, He acts in grace to save us. "The grace of God that brings salvation hath appeared to all men" (Titus 2:11). Paul wrote, "For by grace are we saved through faith" (Eph. 2:8).

In response to the grace of God we should be thankful and live for God. "By the grace of God I am what I am, and His grace which was bestowed upon me was not in vain, for I labor more abundantly than they all: yet not I, but the grace of God which was with me" (1 Cor. 15:16). We should grow stronger in grace because God's goodness has been shown to us. "But grow in grace, and in the knowledge of our Lord and Savior Jesus Christ" (2 Pet. 3:18).

A third attribute of God's goodness is seen in the benevolent supply He gives for the welfare of mankind. Jesus tells us God's benevolence extends to all people. "He makes the sun to rise on the evil and the good and sends rain on the just and the unjust" (Matt. 5:45).

Paul used the good benevolent nature of God as a reason why people should get saved. "He is . . . good, and gave us rain from heaven, and fruitful seasons, filling our hearts with food and gladness" (Acts 14:17).

Finally, the goodness of God is seen in His "longsuffering," or patience. God should have destroyed mankind because of Adam's sin, but He didn't. God is good in that He waits for people to repent and turn to Him (see Rom. 2:4). "The Lord is slow to anger and great in mercy" (Ps. 145:8).

God's longsuffering is the patience whereby His love and goodness overshadow His holiness and judgment. "The Lord . . . is longsuffering to us, not willing that any should perish, but that all should come to repentance" (2 Pet. 3:9).

What should be our response to God's goodness? Because God is good, and because He has given us the goodness of salvation, we should "hold fast that which is good" (1 Thess. 5:20). We should do "good works" (Matt. 5:16) and "depart from evil and do good" (Ps. 27:27).

My Time to Pray

Lord, you are good and merciful to me; thank You for Your grace and kindness in giving me salvation.
Help me live a godly life of holiness, and to be a testimony of Your grace. Lord, You are good, gracious, merciful and kind.
I worship You for Your longsuffering of me.
I will live righteously for You.
Amen.

37

God Has
Person-like Traits

*Christ is the brightness of the Father's glory and
the perfect image of His person.*
HEBREWS 1:3, *ELT*

Most religions of the world reflect God as a distant, uninterested power or just a force. Some see God as an impersonal being, just as a plate on a table or a picture on the wall. Others say God is just an idea. But these designations all fall way short of the New Testament description.

So who is God? Can we get to know Him? Zophar, the friend of Job, asked, "Canst thou by searching find out God?" (Job 11:7, *KJV*). The answer is yes! But we must come to Him on His terms. Jeremiah 29:13 says, "You will seek Me and find Me, when you seek Me with all your hearts." We can know God and we can learn about Him through His person-like traits.

For example, we can talk to God in prayer as we talk to other people, because God has all the properties of a person. In other words, He has the power of personality. We don't project onto God our power of personality. The opposite is true; we get our personality from God.

"God said, 'Let us make man in Our image' " (Gen. 1:26). When you see yourself in the mirror each morning, what do you see? You see an exact reflection of yourself. But when God looks into our face, He sees an image of Himself. Not physically, but God sees us as a person who can think, feel and make decisions, just as He can. Of course, our characteristics are much more finite, while God's characteristics are infinite.

God is wise in creation (see Prov. 3:14), wise in preserving life (see Neh. 9:6), wise in His providence (see Eph. 1:11) and wise in redemption (see Eph. 1:7). Since intelligence is essential to personality, and God is infinite, we must conclude that God has infinite intelligence.

God has a mind (see Gen. 18:19; Exod. 3:7). He remembers (see Gen. 8:1). He reasons (see Isa. 1:18). Speech is based on our recall of word symbols, and God does that. And because God has a mind to think, He has created rationality in us. Now God expects us to think our thought after His direction.

God has emotions, so He created the passion of life into us. We love our mother, pizza and our free time. God grieves (see Gen. 6:6), loves (see John 3:16), is kind (see Ps. 103:8-13), empathizes with people (see Exod. 3:7-8), feels sorrow (see John 11:35) and gets angry at evil (see Ps. 7:11). Yet of all God's emotions, His love is most powerful and best known. He loves perfectly because He is perfect. He loves because of His nature; that is who He is. *Lord, thank You for loving me.*

The ultimate act of personality is the ability to make decisions that give direction to one's life. God has the power of volition, which means He has the freedom and ability to make decisions, so God created into us the ability to make choices and to direct our life by good decisions. At times He makes decisions based on what He knows, and at other times, He chooses out of His love or His hatred for sin and disobedience. Still, at other times, God makes decisions out of His volitional nature.

However, since God is a person, He acts as a unit. Therefore, the will of God is the natural extension of what He thinks, feels and desires.

God is a person with self-perception or the power to know Himself. He told Moses, "I AM THAT I AM" (Exod. 3:14), which means God has self-awareness. He is aware of who He is and is aware of what He can do.

When God told Moses, "I will be with you" (Exod. 3:12), God was exercising self-direction. Thousands of times throughout Scripture God said "I will," meaning that God has self-determination. God is free to do what He chooses.

All of these aspects demonstrate that God has personality. He has a mind to think, emotions to feel deeply and volition to choose to do His will. God has self-perception and self-direction.

God can do whatever He chooses to do.
God has not chosen to do everything.
When God has chosen to do anything,
nothing can stop Him.
God chooses at times not to do everything He can do.
God honors the free will He has given to people.

Some ask the question, "Can we rightly call God a person?" That's an excellent question because the word *person* is so small and limiting. We think of those we know with personality, and we think of a winsome personality or a belligerent personality. To us, personality is a limiting word, and God is so much greater than personality. To think of Him is to think of mysteries, majesty and power. Yes, God is a person, which is at the very core of who He is, but He is much greater and much more majestic.

My Time to Pray

Lord, I come to You, knowing You hear me when I pray,
You love me because of Your nature, and
You have chosen a plan for my life.
Lord, I come to worship You and praise Your name;
You have done so much for me.
But the greatest thing is that You know me intimately;
God, You let me know You in return.
Lord, I reach out to touch You with my worship,
But more importantly, touch me with Your presence.
Amen.

38

God Is All-Powerful

For with God nothing shall be impossible.
LUKE 1:37, KJV

With God all things are possible.
MATTHEW 19:26

God can do everything that He wants to do; nothing is impossible to Him. He created this vast and powerful universe just by speaking what He wanted done. But that's only a small aspect of what He has power to do. God is omnipotent, meaning He has all power, greater than anything we've ever seen.

The speed of His planets is awesome. The burning intensity of the fiery stars is majestic. Their size is mind-boggling. The sun is over one million times larger than our small earth where we live. In the next galaxy is Antares, which is 64 million times greater than our sun. In another galaxy is Hercules, which is 110 million times the size of Antares. Finally there is Epsilon, several million times larger than any other star. *Lord, You are infinite, without limitations and all-powerful.*

This vast universe is beyond our comprehension, yet the creation of just one man was so much greater. When we consider our smallness in comparison to the universe, we cry out with the psalmist, "When I observe Your heavens, the work of Your fingers, the moon and the stars You set in place, what is man that You remember him . . . ?" (Ps. 8:3-4, *CSB*).

God's power is seen in the small, intricate things that we humans can observe but could never achieve on our own. God can imbed DNA in every molecule, and He poured His mighty power into an atom of protons, neutrons and electrons, with the electrons swirling around the nucleus with awesome nuclear force.

God can raise the dead, walk on water and count the hairs on your head and the head of the six billion souls on the earth. He does all this without effort. What God wills is carried out (see Isa. 59:1-2).

We can see and understand God's power. He didn't withhold it nor did He hide it. The *Today's English Version* of the Bible puts it this way: "Ever since God created the world, His invisible qualities, both His eternal power and His divine nature have been clearly seen. Men can perceive them in the things that God has made" (Rom. 1:20, *TEV*).

Things God Can't Do
God can't make a square circle.
God can't make yesterday not happen.
God can't see a thing that's not there.
God can't deny His existence (see 2 Tim. 2:13).
God can't lie (see Heb. 6:18).
God can't be tempted to sin (see Jas. 1:13).

God's power holds everything together: "By Him all things hold together" (Col. 1:17, *CSB*). When we see the almost limitless power of a nuclear explosion when the atom is split, it forces us to ask, "What holds all the trillions times trillions times trillions of atoms together?" The answer? God's power.

There are things God can't do. God can't do impossible or absurd things, such as make 2 + 2 = 3. Also, God can't do things that are contrary to His nature, such as create sin.

God can do whatever He wills to do, but He does not necessarily will to do everything. God could have exercised His power to keep sin out of the world, but that would have been inconsistent with His will to allow people created in His image to exercise their free will. Because we are created in the image of God who has free will, He has allowed us to exercise our free will. Why? Because God wants honest worship. Remember, authentic worship and fellowship are only authentic when praise flows freely from one who chooses to magnify God. If we talked like those baby dolls with recording devices to say only what it was manufactured to say, then our praise would mean little to God. *Lord, I choose to love You and worship You.*

When Eve ate the fruit and sinned, God could have destroyed Satan and evil, but He allows sin and Satan to exist. So in our continued testing, we demonstrate our love to God by choosing to obey Him. Therefore an all-powerful God limits His power in keeping within the purpose of His will for us. *Lord, I will find Your will for my life and do it.*

Because God reigns over His universe, His power makes everything accomplish His perfect will. So God is sovereign over things seen and unseen, over the material world and the unseen spiritual world. But most of all, God has power over us who are made in His image. To those who believe in God, ask for forgiveness and obey Him, for God has the power to "work all things for good" (Rom. 8:28).

My Time to Pray

Lord, Your power and majesty are great,
Beyond anything I can comprehend.
I worship You and praise You,
For I am fearfully and wonderfully made.
Lord, You can do everything You desire.
Be merciful and gracious to me;
I am just a servant of Yours.
Amen.

39

God Is All-Knowing

Great is our Lord, and of great power: His understanding is infinite.
PSALM 147:5, *KJV*

The only wise God.
JUDE 25, *KJV*

We may strive to know God, but our knowledge pales in comparison to the knowledge that God has. He knows all things, past, present and future, and understands all things from the most complex scientific processes to the innermost thoughts of our souls. How is this possible?

Since God is eternal, He was present when everything was created, so He has knowledge of all things since the beginning. He has never had to learn anything. Also, since God is not limited to time, He exists in the past, the present and the future. Therefore, God can't forget anything since He was living when everything happened in the past. God has all knowledge.

Since God is omnipresent, meaning God is present everywhere at the same time, He knows all things because everything happens or exists within His presence no matter where or when they occur.

The word "infinite" means "without limits." Since God is infinite, He is not limited by space, time, power or knowledge. He knows and understands the sum total of all knowledge and wisdom. He even knows those things mankind has yet to discover. Nothing surprises God.

Since God is wise, He knows the potential of everything that might have happened but didn't occur. The Bible says He "calleth those things which be not as though they were" (Rom. 4:17, *KJV*), which suggests that God is wise enough to know what would have happened to you if you took an alternative of every decision you've ever faced.

When I (Elmer) was going through Bible college, I tended to check out all the girls on campus as a potential wife. As men are apt to do, I usually chose the ones I thought were good-looking, smart and had a "bouncy" personality. In God's sovereignty, I chose Ruth Forbes, actually the best looking, smartest and, thankfully, the most spiritual of all the girls in our freshmen class.

God knows what would have happened to me if I married any one of those other girls. When I think of being married to some of the other girls—those I probably prayed for—I shudder with fear to think of the mistake I might have made. Continually I praise God for His choice for my life. God is wise and good. *Lord, thank You for every good decision You've led me to make.*

It is important to realize that God has not learned all these things. If we say that God learned, we would be saying that He did not know something in the past and that would make Him imperfect and less than God. But this is not the case. Instead He knows everything before it happens to us or before we learn it. The prophet Isaiah asks, "Who has directed the Spirit of the Lord, or as His counselor has taught Him? With whom did He take counsel, and who instructed Him, and taught Him in the path of justice? Who taught Him knowledge, and showed Him the way of understanding?" (Isa. 40:13-14). The answer? No one! Therefore, God has never had to learn anything.

God also knows all things equally well. Some people know a few things about a lot of different topics. Other people have a great amount of knowledge about a specific area, but God's knowledge and understanding are infinite in everything. "Everything in all creation is exposed and lies open before His eyes" (Heb. 4:13, *TEV*).

Consider this one area: There are trillions and trillions of stars, and every day it seems scientists are finding new stars and galaxies never before seen or known to mankind. But the scientists are wrong in saying new stars are being created; it's just that they are finding those stars that already exist. In the psalms, David recounts, "He counts the number of the stars; He calls them all by name. Great is our Lord, and mighty in power; His understanding is infinite" (Ps. 147:4). God already knows the exact number of stars and has a name for each.

And that's only a small glimpse of His infinite knowledge! Whatever an infinite mind knows, only an infinite mind understands, for only an unlimited mind has unlimited understanding. Because we are limited, we can never fully know God, but what we do know about Him should cause us to worship Him for His greatness. *Lord, I worship Your greatness and majesty.*

Finally, since God knows everything, we can have confidence that He has a plan for our lives. *Lord, I trust Your future for me.* "I know the plans I have for you," says the Lord. "They are plans for good and not for disaster, to give you a future and a hope" (Jer. 29:11, *TLB*). Since God knows you and knows your future, wouldn't you like for Him to lead you today? Wouldn't you like for the Lord to show you His will for your life? *Lord, I wait for Your leading.*

When we talk about the omniscience of God, we mean He possesses perfect knowledge of all things. The prefix "omni" means "all" and the word "science" comes from a Latin root meaning "knowledge." The omniscient God has all knowledge in this world and in eternity. His knowledge is infinite, which means "without limits" of time, space or topic. God knows all things, from the solutions to the world's most complex problems to the quiet ponderings of our hearts.

My Time to Pray

Lord, I praise You for Your infinite wisdom and knowledge.
I trust You to lead me in this life.
I know You have a good plan for my life;
Your plan is better than anything I can conceive.
Lord, I trust You to guide me in all decisions.
I need Your wisdom and direction.
Amen.

40

God Is Present Everywhere

I can never get away from your presence! If I go to heaven,
you are there; if I go down to the place of the dead, you are there.
If I ride the wings of the morning, if I dwell in the farthest oceans,
even there your hand will guide me.
PSALM 139:7-9, *NLT*

The theologians have said God is present everywhere at the same time. They called this the *omnipresence* of God. The prefix "omni" means "all," so God is present at all places. The word "presence" means "here," so God is here and everywhere else.

The omnipresence of God demonstrates His immensity. In other words, since God is present everywhere at the same time, He is big—really big. God exists in every place at every time. In the book of Psalms, David writes, "I can't get away from God, He's everywhere" (Ps. 139:7). Even when you travel to the last star and jump off into the blackness of nothingness, God is in the blackness of nothing. God is infinite, without limits or boundaries. Does God's presence have a center? Technically, His center is everywhere. Even David said, "Where can I flee from Your presence?" (Ps. 139:7). The answer, of course, is nowhere.

But what about after Cain killed Abel, where the Bible says, "Cain went out from the presence of the Lord" (Gen. 4:16)? How did Cain leave God if God is everywhere? The truth is that Cain couldn't get away from the presence of God; Cain only left the place of God's blessing and usefulness.

There are several ways to describe the presence of the Lord. First, there is the *localized presence* of God, where God makes His presence known in an actual, physical location. God was present in the Shekinah glory cloud that covered the tabernacle of meeting when He led the Israelites through the wilderness (see Exod. 40:34-38). When God spoke from heaven at the baptism of Jesus, He said, "This is My beloved Son in whom I am well pleased" (Matt. 3:17), which also demonstrated God's localized presence. God localized Himself to help us understand His ministry to us and to focus our worship on Him.

Second, God's presence can also be an *indwelling presence*. When we are saved, Christ comes to dwell in our hearts. Galatians 2:20 says, "I have been crucified with Christ and I no longer live, but Christ lives in me." God the Father can also indwell us (see John 14:23) as well as the Holy Spirit (see John 14:17). As a child of God, it's comforting to know that God lives in us. *Lord, I will be a good testimony because I carry You wherever I go.*

Third, God can manifest Himself as an *institutional presence*. Just as God dwelt in the Holy of Holies in the Tabernacle, Jesus comes to live in His institution, the Church (see Matt. 16:18). God promises us that "where two or three are gathered together in My name, I am there in the midst of them" (Matt. 18:20).

Sometimes I (Elmer) walk into a church meeting and can feel the presence of the Lord. I know God is working in hearts and His *institutional presence* in the church motivates me to preach the Word with boldness.

Then, too, I have been invited to preach in churches that are cold and dead. I don't feel the presence of the Lord in their services. Those churches need revival. Just as when a person faints and he needs to be revived, so too some churches have fainted and need to be revived.

Revival comes when God brings His presence to His people. In Peter's sermon in Acts, God says, "I will pour out my Spirit in those days" to bring revival to the church (Acts 2:18). Sometimes I (Charles) have been leading worship and I can actually feel God pouring Himself on the people as they sing. How do I know it's God's presence and not just stirred up emotions or mass hysteria? God says He will come to sit on the throne in the middle of people praising Him. "But You are holy, enthroned in the praises of Israel" (Ps. 22:3). What I am experiencing is a small taste of revival. *Lord, pour out Your Spirit on my heart.*

Finally, there is God's *omnipresence*, which means He is present everywhere at the same time. This omnipresence means that He sees all and knows all. Hagar wisely said, "You are the God who sees me" (Gen. 16:13).

So is God in the tavern where people are getting drunk? Yes, so don't do it in God's presence. Is God in the bedroom where a couple is committing adultery? Yes, so don't do it in God's presence. God is present where every sin is committed, where every lie is told and wherever His name is blasphemed. *Lord, when You see things in my life that displease You, forgive me.*

My Time to Pray

Lord, I know You are everywhere present today.
I know You are in my life;
Let me feel Your presence today.
Lord, You are already present everywhere I go,
So protect me in every situation
That I encounter in my life today.
I know You love me and protect me,
So wrap Yourself around me wherever I go.
I know You have a great plan for my life;
Guide me to do Your perfect will today.
Amen.

41

God Is Spirit

God is Spirit, and those who worship Him
must worship in spirit and truth.
JOHN 4:24

Throughout the Bible, God is called *spirit*. Though corrected in the *New King James Version*, the original *King James Version* wrongly translated this verse, "God is a spirit" (John 4:24, *KJV*). In fact, God does not have a spirit; He *is* spirit in nature. But God is not like a spirit as the world defines—the spirit of capitalism, the spirit of St. Louis or a ghost that some call a spirit. No! God is spirit in nature. But what does this mean?

When you say that God is spirit, you are saying that God is immaterial and invisible. When the religions of the world make an idol, they are limiting God so they can get a hand on Him. So God told us, "You shall not make for yourself a carved image—any likeness of anything that is in heaven above, or that is in the earth beneath, or that is in the water under the earth; you shall not bow down to them nor serve them" (Exod. 20:4-5).

Although His spirit nature is immaterial and invisible, God is said to have hands (see Isa. 65:2), feet (see Ps. 18:9), eyes (see 1 Kings 8:29) and fingers (see Exod. 8:29). But these are not to be understood as actual physical parts of God. They are "anthropomorphisms," whereby we project physical characteristics on God to help us understand that God does the functions of these physical parts.

To understand God as spirit is also to realize He can be omnipresent, or present everywhere at the same time. This not only means His spirit nature can be in every geographic location simultaneously, but also in every time—past, present and future—all at once.

There are times in the Bible when people said they saw God (see Gen. 32:20), or they saw a manifestation of God (see Exod. 3:6; 29:9-10; Isa. 6:1). In fact, they didn't actually see God; they saw the reflection or *spirit* of God. They saw the results of God, but they didn't actually see God directly. God was in the pillar that led Israel through the wilderness and they saw the cloud of fire that hid God, but they didn't see God (see Deut. 4:15). "No man has seen God at any time" (John 1:18).

Individuals saw God physically for the first time when they saw Jesus in the flesh. "No one has seen God at any time" (John 1:18). John wrote to reinforce this truth, and later declared, "I myself have seen Him with my own eyes, and listened to Him speak. I have touched Him with my own hands. He is God's messenger of life" (1 John 1:1, *ELT*).

Paul wrote, "When the fullness of time had come, God sent forth His Son" (Gal. 4:4). Even though we can't see God in the flesh, we can see Jesus in the Scriptures. We know how Jesus was born, how He lived, what miracle He did, and how He died for us. Our hearts can know Him experientially, as if we touch Him with our fingers.

My Time to Pray

Lord, You are a spirit without physical form,
Yet I see You in my heart when I pray.
I trace Your image in the pages of Scripture.
You are everywhere present in Your universe.
I hear Your voice in the wind,
And I see Your fingerprint in the Blue Ridge Mountains.
Lord, You manifest Yourself in the Scriptures
And when I can't see You with my physical eyes,
Then I see You in my heart.
Amen.

42

God Never Changes

For I am the Lord, I do not change.
MALACHI 3:6

We change constantly. We change our minds, change our views and change our preferences. Our bodies, knowledge and hairstyles all change. But God never changes. God's nature is ultimate perfection in all He is, says and does, and it never has, or will, change from this perfection. Therefore if God is perfect and He's never changed, He hasn't gotten better over time, nor will He get better in the future.

The same can be said for God getting worse than He is. God is not an old man who loses His strength, His ability to concentrate or His ability to do things. God has embodied perfection since the beginning of time and He has not changed.

The unchanging nature of God is often called His immutability. "For I am the Lord, I do not change" (Mal. 3:6). How do we know God is immutable? The Bible provides a number of examples of His steadfastness.

God is unchanging in His existence. Psalm 90:2 proclaims, "Before the mountains were born or you brought forth the earth and the world, from everlasting to everlasting you are God." God always has been and always will be in existence (see

Deut. 32:39-40; Pss. 9:7; 55:60; 102:12; Hab. 1:12; 1 Tim. 1:17; 6:16). *Lord, I trust in Your presence because You've always been there and always will be.*

God is unchanging in His justice. Zephaniah 3:5 reads, "The LORD is righteous in her midst, He will do no unrighteousness. Every morning He brings His justice to light; He never fails." Since God's nature demands that He judge sin and He is immutable, He can't change His mind about punishing those sinners who reject His Son. *Lord, thank You that Jesus died for my sin and forgave me.*

Thankfully, God is also unchanging in His mercy (see Deut. 7:9; 1 Chron. 16:34). The psalms read, "Oh, give thanks to the LORD, for He is good! For His mercy endures forever" (Ps. 106:1). Though God's justice is fixed, His mercy has no limit. It never runs out, never runs dry and covers all of our sins. *Thank You for Your unending mercy and forgiveness.*

God is unchanging in His holiness. "I am the LORD your God; consecrate yourselves and be holy, because I am holy" (Lev. 11:44). The word "holy" means "to be set apart." From beginning to end, God has been set apart, pure and unblemished. *Lord, I praise Your unending holiness.*

God is unchanging in His truth and His knowledge. In the psalms, David calls out, "Redeem me, O LORD, God of truth" (Ps. 31:5), and writes that "the LORD is good; his mercy is everlasting; and his truth endures to all generations" (Ps. 100:5). Later in chapter 139, David praises God for His knowledge: "Before a word is on my tongue you know it completely, O LORD . . . All the days ordained for me were written in your book before one of them came to be" (Ps. 139:4,16). *Lord, thank You that Your truth is everlasting and that You know me inside and out.*

In addition to God's immutable nature, His love and promises are also unchanging. Not only did God love His people so much that He sent His Son to die for their sins (see John

3:16), but He also has always loved them (see Ps. 107:1) and wants all of them to be saved (see 2 Pet. 3:9). *God, thank You for loving me eternally.*

In the same way, we can have confidence in God's unchanging promises: "Know therefore that the LORD your God is God; he is the faithful God, keeping his covenant of love to a thousand generations of those who love him and keep his commands" (Deut. 7:9). Since God's promises are immutable, I can rest in His pledge to me (see Rom. 4:21). *Lord, thank You for the strength of Your promises.*

"Immutability" is another word to describe God's unchanging nature. We can have confidence in the immutability of God's existence, justice, mercy, holiness, truth, knowledge, love and promises to us. When things around us seem to change from day to day or buckle under the pressures of the world, we can stand firm in our faith, knowing that our God is steadfast.

My Time to Pray

Lord, I thank You for Your unchangeableness.
You've been the same throughout my life.
You've been the same throughout eternity.
I thank You for Your love and goodness to me;
You have given me much more than I deserve.
Lord, I worship You as my rock and my strength,
When I change, You change not.
When I sin and confess my iniquity to You,
You forgive me as You promised to do.
Amen.

43

God Is Three in One

The grace of our Lord Jesus Christ, and the love of God, and the
communion of the Holy Spirit, be with you all, amen.
2 CORINTHIANS 13:14

I (Elmer) can be three different persons in one morning. As an author, I study in the morning, writing my notes or an article from the things I discover in my research. Then I take the children and grandchildren out to lunch, taking the smaller ones to the dollar store and inviting them to get anything they want. In this playful role, I'm a grandparent. Later for exercise I play nine holes as a golfer. Author, grandparent and golfer—all in one morning.

Yet this is a poor illustration of the Trinity of the Father, Son and Holy Spirit, because it's only one person *doing* three things. In the Trinity, there are three distinct and separate persons. The Athanasian Creed, one of the oldest creeds of the Christian faith, says of the Trinity, "We worship one God in Trinity, and Trinity in unity; neither confounding the persons, nor dividing the substance."

The Father, Son and Holy Spirit are three distinct persons who exist together in unity as the Trinity. Each member of the Trinity is God, and each has voluntarily adopted submissive roles to each other.

How are they submissive to each other? The Son, the second person of the Trinity, is eternally begotten by the Father (see Ps. 2:7), and the Holy Spirit is described as eternally proceeding from the Father and Son (see John 15:26).

Each member of the Trinity is full God, yet they exist in Unity. They are separate in person, equal in nature, and submissive to one another in duties.

We can also try to understand the triune nature of God by thinking about the people it takes to build a house. The Father is the architect-engineer who plans the house design. The Son is the contractor who goes on the site (the earth) to do the work of construction. The Holy Spirit is the worker who actually does the physical work. Each needs the other and all three must work together in unison for the project to be complete.

Sometimes it is easier to understand the Trinity by looking at what the Trinity is not. The Trinity is not three Gods (tritheism). Christians are monotheists, meaning they believe in one God. "Hear O Israel: the Lord our God is one Lord" (Deut. 6:4). So, we don't believe in three Gods.

Also, the Trinity is not three different manifestations of one God. *Modalism* teaches that the Old Testament Father *becomes* the Son, who in turn *becomes* the Holy Spirit. The basic error of modalism is that it denies the distinctiveness of each person of the godhead, and it denies the eternality of each of the three persons. God is not sometimes the Father, sometimes the Son and sometimes the Holy Spirit. He is all three, all the time.

Also, the Son and the Holy Spirit are not mere attributes or influences of the Father. The Bible teaches that Jesus was God: "In the beginning was the Word, and the Word was with God, and the Word was God" (John 1:1). Then it says, "The Word became flesh"

(John 1:14), meaning that Jesus the Word became a person. So the Son is not just a characteristic of God; He is a person of God.

A number of examples of the triune nature of God can be found in the Bible. The way God talked with Himself in Scripture reflects the Trinity. There was a plurality among the Godhead in the beginning when God said, "Let *us* make man in our image" (Gen. 1:26, emphasis added). When the Godhead appeared to Isaiah, they said, "Who will go for *us*?" (Isa. 6:8, emphasis added).

Another clear example of the Trinity can be seen in the baptism of Jesus as recorded in Matthew. After Jesus was baptized in the Jordan River, the Father from heaven says, "This is my Son in whom I am well pleased," and the Holy Spirit in the form of a dove descends on Jesus (Matt. 3:16-17). All three persons of God—Father, Son and Holy Spirit—are present for the event.

The Early Church also worshiped in a trinitarian formula: "The grace of our Lord Jesus Christ, and the love of God, and the communion of the Holy Spirit be with you all" (2 Cor. 13:14).

As further proof, look at the way Jesus instructed us to baptize a new convert: "In the name of the Father, and of the Son, and of the Holy Spirit" (Matt. 28:19).

Finally, one of the strongest proofs of the Trinity is that the Bible reveals that each member of the Trinity possesses the same attributes and tasks of the other members.

The Attributes of the Trinity

ATTRIBUTES	FATHER	SON	HOLY SPIRIT
Omnipresence	Jer. 23:24	Matt. 28:20	Ps. 139:7-12
Omnipotence	Rom. 1:16	Matt. 28:18	Rom. 15:19
Omniscience	Rom. 11:33	John 21:17	John 14:26
Immutability	Mal. 3:6	Heb. 13:8	Hag. 2:5
Eternality	Ps. 90:2	John 1:1	Heb. 9:14
Holiness	Lev. 19:2	Heb. 4:15	name "Holy"
Love	1 John 3:1	Matt. 9:36	name "Holy"

The Work of the Trinity

WORK	FATHER	SON	HOLY SPIRIT
Creation of world	Ps. 102:25	John 1:3	Gen. 1:2
Creation of man	Gen. 2:7	Col. 1:16	Job 33:4
Death of Christ	Isa. 53:10	John 10:18	Heb. 9:14
Resurrection of Christ	Acts 2:32	John 2:19	1 Pet. 3:18
Inspiration	Heb. 1:1-2	1 Pet. 1:10-11	2 Pet. 1:21
Indwelling of believers	Col. 1:7	1 Cor. 6:19	Eph. 4:6
Authority of ministry	2 Cor. 3:4-6	1 Tim. 1:12	Acts 20:28
Security of believer	John 10:29	Phil. 1:6	Eph. 1:13-14

Christians believe in one God in three Persons: Father, Son and Holy Spirit. Each member of the Trinity is God and each works in our lives today. Lord, I want Your work in my life.

As God, each member of the Godhead is worthy of our worship and deserving of our obedience. They have each revealed themselves in Scripture, and expect us to respond accordingly. *Lord, it is my desire to love, worship and obey You, the triune God.*

My Time to Pray

Lord, I worship You, Father, Son and Holy Spirit.
I cry holy, holy, holy to You
The Three in One, eternal God.
Lord, early in the morning I will come to You,
Praying for Your blessing on my life
And waiting for Your grace.
Lord, I will worship You, Father, for Your love and mercy;
I praise You, Jesus, for salvation;
I thank You, Holy Spirit, for working in my life.
Amen.

Epilogue

So, God laughs? Isn't laughing something we all enjoy doing? When we find out that God laughs, doesn't that make us like God even more? But God doesn't do the things we do; it's the other way around. We do the things we do because we were originally created in God's image. So God was the first to laugh, sing, whisper, hate or frown.

Therefore, the more you learn about God, the more you will better know yourself. And the opposite is true: the better you understand yourself, the better you will understand God.

But wait! What about our sin, our addictions and our rebellion? What about crime, murder, blasphemy and theft? Where does that come from? Does sin come from God? The answer is no! Sin began when Adam and Eve disobeyed God in the Garden of Eden. They received a sin nature that produced more disobedience in every area of life, and that sin nature was passed on to all people (see Rom. 5:12).

Every person has two natures within. First, they have a sinful nature that makes them sin. Then they have a good nature from God that makes them do good things. Therefore, the secret to understanding life is to get to know God so you can do good things in the power of God. That's why Charles and I wrote this book: to give you the key to better living.

I (Elmer) once sat next to a well-dressed businessman as I was flying out of Pittsburgh, Pennsylvania. In talking with him, I found out that he had a Doctor of Law degree from a prestigious law school, but that he was now president of a large manufacturing plant. When he asked me what I did and where I worked, I told him that I was a professor in the School of Religion at Liberty University.

Suddenly, everything changed. The man became combative, telling me he was an atheist and that he had no time for God. He cursed Jerry Falwell and "every idiot who believes in creation and Adam and Eve." He hated our stand on right to life, homosexuality and moral purity. He began to build a case—in lawyer-type debate style—for evolution. He used the phrase "laws of evolution" several times, explaining that the power of the universe comes from the laws of evolution.

After listening to him "preach" his liberal worldview, I asked a question: "If all life comes from the laws of evolution, what is the source of law?"

He sat stunned. Silence! I let it sink in, and then I asked, "Who was the first law giver?"

He had no answer.

Who was the first Law Giver? The answer is God. Everything comes from God the Creator. All natural laws, such as the laws of nature that we teach in biology, chemistry and calculus, come from God. Everything, including the laws of personality that we teach in psychology, sociology and anthropology, come from Him as well.

Study again all the things about God you didn't know. There is no God like our God. No world religion has a god like our God. He is everything the normal rational mind would expect Him to be.

Study Guide

Prepared by Nathan Lorick

God Laughs is a study of some of the uncommon characteristics that we might not know about God, along with some of the more expected aspects of what makes God who He is. The purpose of this book is to help you reflect on the heart of God, because when you know God better, you can worship Him better and serve Him better.

This study guide has been prepared to help you understand and embrace some of these surprising things about God as well as some of the more well-known things about Him. If you are using this study in a small-group setting, be sure that each member has a personal copy of the book and reads through the assigned chapters before the session begins. The pastor or study leader can use the questions and faith challenges to guide group members through a better understanding of God as found in the book. The pastor or leader should help group members make practical application of the aspects of God as they learn them in the book.

Session One: God Is Love

CHAPTERS TO READ: 6, 8, 14, 23, 24, 34

God is love, and understanding the vastness of that love will help us to better realize the sacrifice He made for us through Jesus Christ. This, in turn, will help us to see our lives with His love as the backdrop. This should lead us to experience and express His love to others.

1. In chapter 34, the authors write, "To say that God is love makes Christianity unique among the religions of the world." How does this relate to you as you strive to be a Christian in a world that is continually rejecting God's love? In what ways can you show others that the God of Christianity does everything on the basis of love? How can you communicate that God's love is completely different from any other religious figure?

2. In chapter 6, the authors state that God thinks about us constantly and that we are never out of His mind. How does it make you feel to know that you are constantly on the mind of God? Does this change the way you think about Him? Does this express to you the significance of God's love for you?

3. As the authors relate in chapters 8 and 23, although God anguishes over our sins, He chooses not to remember them after we confess them to Him and seek His forgiveness. Are you able to see God's love in His decision to no longer remember your sins once you confess them to Him? Should this cause you to forgive others and remember their trespasses against you no longer? How does the fact that God does not remember our past sins relate to His love for us?

4. In chapter 24, the authors write, "Just as water quenches our bodily thirst, so too fellowship with God quenches the yearnings of the soul." In what ways are you and your church seeking to quench the needs in your community and communicate God's love? Do people see God's love through your life? Do they see God's love through your church?

5. Do you feel that people understand God's love by watching the way you live your life? Do you understand the sacrifices of God's love for you? Does this affect your life daily?

6. What are some practical ways that you can show God's love to your family, your friends, your neighbors and your co-workers? Will they be able to connect the dots between your deeds and God's love?

7. In chapter 14, the authors state, "God loves to provide for His people, but notice that His provision is based on *relationship*. . . . You must obey if you want God's provision." In what ways have you experienced God's love through His provision? Have you ever seen God provide in abundance? Are you living in obedience to God so that you may experience His provision?

FAITH CHALLENGE

1. Make a list of the times that you have experienced God's love in your life. On this list, document your circumstances and reflect on the times in which you felt closer to God because of the love that He showed to you.

2. Take a week and study John 3:16. Meditate on what it means for God to love you with such passion and sacrifice. Make a list of the things in your life that hinder you from daily experiencing and expressing God's love.

3. Make a commitment today to show God's love to others. Make sure that you are living your life in obedience to God's

will so that others may see Jesus through you. Try to impact five people this week with an act of kindness that communicates God's love.

Session Two: God Is Holy

CHAPTERS TO READ: 2, 16, 20, 26, 27, 35

To understand God's sovereignty, we must first understand His holiness. God is holy because of who He is. His holiness is something that we are to strive to attain. In fact, He tells us to mirror His example and to be holy (see Lev. 11:44-45; 1 Pet. 1:16). His holiness should lead us to be set apart in our lives for His glory.

1. In chapter 35, the authors quote the following from A. W. Tozer: "We cannot grasp the true meaning of divine holiness . . . it stands apart, unique, unapproachable, incomprehensible, and unattainable. The natural man is blind to it." By what standard do you measure holiness? Do you rely on a pastor, a Sunday School teacher, a hero of the Bible—or do you hold God as the only standard of personal holiness? Does God's holiness give you a desire for personal holiness?

2. In grasping God's holiness, we must also see that because He is holy there are things He hates. In chapter 16, the authors state that God absolutely hates selfish pride: "These seven things that God hates deal with inward sins of the heart, not outward sins. Our inward motives always determine our outward actions; our inward selfish pride is the source of our sin that God hates." What are some things in

your life that show evidence of selfish pride? What are some things in your church that are more focused on the congregation than on God's glory? What are some things you can do to change the selfish focus in your life or in your church?

3. Not only does God hate certain things, but He also gets angry. In chapter 20, the authors state that God "has standards of holiness, and when people break His laws or principles, He becomes angry at their sin." God gets jealous when we put things ahead of our relationship with Him, and He punishes our sin (see chapters 26 and 27). What are some of the things that have taken the place of God in your life? What are some things that have happened in your church that have angered God? In what ways have you seen God punish sin? Because God's anger is a sign of His love for us, how can we show God's love to others through His anger?

4. In chapter 2, the authors state, "Because God is holy, when we meditate on Him, we will slowly become holy like God." However, sin that is not confessed can keep us from attaining the holiness that God desires in our lives. Is there sin in your life that has not been confessed? Are you clinging to something in your life that is detrimental to your personal holiness? If so, what will you do about it today?

5. God not only desires for individuals to be holy, but He also desires for believers corporately to be holy. What are some areas of your church that could be improved upon in order to better mirror the holiness of God? Is there a need for reconciliation? What are some ways that your church can communicate God's holiness to unholy people?

FAITH CHALLENGE

1. Take a week and study some of the Scriptures that deal with God's holiness (e.g., Exod. 15:11; Lev. 11:44-45; 20:7,26; 21:8; 22:32; Pss. 24:3; 77:13; 99:9; Isa. 5:16; Rom. 6:19; 7:12; 12:1; 2 Pet. 3:11; Rev. 4:8). Meditate on what God's desire for you to be holy means in your day-to-day life. Make a list of things in your life that you need to eliminate in order to pursue personal holiness.

2. Seek out anyone in your life who you need to forgive or from whom you need to receive forgiveness. Contact that person and seek reconciliation. Express your desire for holiness and unity.

Session Three: God Is Good

CHAPTERS TO READ: 11, 17, 18, 30, 31, 36

God is good all the time, and all the time God is good. God reveals His goodness to us in many ways, and His goodness should motivate us to be good to others. We have the ability to show others the love of God by living out the goodness of God in us.

1. As the authors relate in chapter 36, God's goodness is expressed through His mercy, grace, benevolence and patience. How have you experienced God's mercy? What are some times in your life that God's patience was evident? Is your church currently seeing the evidence of God's goodness?

2. In chapter 17, the authors relate how God heals protectively, which is another example of God's goodness to us. As the authors state, "God has compassion for His chil-

dren. He wants us to live healthy lives of worship and service. God never planned to save the souls of His children
and neglect their physical bodies." Have you ever experienced God's healing? If so, in what ways? Has God revealed
His goodness to you through your health? Are you doing
the necessary things to maintain the goodness of God
through your health?

3. In chapter 18, the authors state that while there is not
much in the Bible that describes God laughing, we do see
that He rejoices over lost people being saved (see Luke
15:10). In this way, we see the goodness of God manifested
in the salvation of people. He laughs and rejoices over each
soul. Reflect on the day of your salvation—the day God re-
joiced over you. Do you remember what it felt like to accept Jesus in your life? Did others know that your life had
been changed? Do people know now that Jesus is real in
you? Is your church seeing God laugh? Are you seeing people receive Jesus? What can you do as a church to hear the
laughter of God more often through peoples' salvation?

4. In chapter 31, the authors use the example of Napoleon and
the lowly lieutenant to illustrate how God displays His
goodness when He is pleased with us. Napoleon's officers
were appalled when the young man asked the general to give
him an island the French army had conquered in the Mediterranean Sea, but they were even more shocked when Napoleon consented. When asked why, Napoleon said, "He
honored me with the magnitude of his request." In the same
way, if we want to please God, we must have as much faith
in our heavenly Father as the lieutenant had in Napoleon.
Does your faith please God and invite His goodness in your
life? Are you pleasing God with what you are doing for Him?
Is His goodness evident in your church through your faith?

5. As the authors state in chapter 11, "God seldom yells to get our attention." God, out of His goodness, whispers to us in a still, small voice. He also satisfies us and gives us strength (see chapter 30). In what ways have you seen evidence of this goodness of God in your life? Is His goodness exercised on a daily basis in you? Are others encountering God's goodness, mercy, grace, benevolence and patience through your life?

FAITH CHALLENGE

1. Write down all of the ways that you have witnessed God's goodness to you in the last month. Think about all the times that God had to be patient with you. Find someone this week to whom you can show the goodness of God.

2. God's goodness is expressed in so many ways, one of which is your health. His goodness for your health coexists with your efforts to maintain a healthy body. So evaluate your health this week. Think of ways in which you can make your body more like the temple it was created to be. In doing this, you will exemplify the goodness of God to others.

Session Four: God Has Person-like Traits

CHAPTERS TO READ: 1, 3, 9, 12, 13, 22, 32, 37

One of the greatest things we know about God is that He has person-like traits. He has the ability to hear us, talk to us, feel our pain, comfort our hurts and love us beyond all comprehension. The fact that God has these traits should lead us to a stronger love for Him and a greater understanding of Him.

1. In chapter 37, the authors explain how God has many person-like traits: He has a mind, He remembers, He reasons. What are some ways that you have seen God exhibit these person-like traits in your life? In what ways has God exhibited these traits to your church? During what times do you most feel God's personhood?

2. The Bible tells us that God has a "nose" (see chapter 12), He has "wax in His ears" (see chapter 13), and even that He whistles (see chapter 22). Another very human-like trait that we see of God is that He has emotions. When do you believe God has been grieved at something you have done? When do you think He expressed love? When do you feel that He was kind to you? When do you think He was angry? Have you ever seen the emotions of God in your church?

3. In chapter 1, the authors state that "God has a heart that reaches out to those He loves." He sees our tears and collects them in a "bottle" (see chapter 32). The fact that God cares for us this deeply and has this person-like trait should make Him even more real to us. Have you ever sought the heart of God? Have you experienced God's heart rejoicing with you? What are evidences that your church is seeking the heart of God? Are you wholeheartedly trying to find the heart of God in your life?

4. In chapter 3, the authors show how God actually sings over us—He sings "because we have done something to make Him rejoice." Are you living your life in such a way that God is singing over you? In what areas of your life or your church would God be singing? Are there areas in which He would not rejoice?

5. In chapter 9, the authors note that "God sees all we do and writes a record in His book." God reads and writes for our benefit! He keeps a record and will one day reveal everything He has written to us. What kind of things is God writing about you? Are these things beneficial or detrimental to the Kingdom? Are you living your life in such a way that God is writing continually in a positive manner? If not, what can you change in your life to make God write with a positive pen?

FAITH CHALLENGE

1. Take a week and study the personal characteristics of God. Meditate on what could cause Him to exhibit these person-like traits. For example, when He sings, why does He sing? Make a list of these characteristics and evaluate how present they are in your life.

2. Spend some time praying this week. Ask God to reveal more of Himself as a person to you. Make a prayer list, asking God to reveal certain personifications to you, and then mark them off your list as He answers each one.

Session Five: God Is All-Powerful

CHAPTERS TO READ: 4, 7, 10, 38

God is all-powerful and cannot be stopped by anything. He has unknowable secrets. He rules and reigns over the entire universe. There is nothing too small or big for Him to do. This should give us confidence that God can and will take care of us in this life.

1. In chapter 38, the authors write, "God is omnipotent, meaning He has all power, greater than anything we've ever seen." What are some areas of your life in which you have witnessed God's power? What is your role in God's power? Do you believe that nothing is too big or small for God? If so, what are some practical things in your life that you need to turn over to God?

2. The mind of God is an indicator of His incredible power. As the authors state in chapter 4, "We can lose our memory, but God can't. He will know all things eternally. He will not forget anything." Your mind is a gift from God. What kinds of things are you doing to use it for Christ? Are you diligent or lazy when it comes to preparing your mind for the things of God? In what ways is God using you according to your usability?

3. While we may not always know the plans of God (see chapter 10), we do know that God does have plans for all individuals, both believers and unbelievers (see chapter 7). God has the power to save people from their sins and give them eternal life. Have you seen this power of God saving someone whom you didn't think would be saved? Have you ever witnessed someone coming into the plans of God out of darkness? Is your church conveying the message that God has a plan for everyone's life through His power?

4. God is eternal—there are no tomorrows for Him. As the authors state in chapter 33, "When you reflect on the heart of God, you'll realize how urgent *today* is. God has given you the gift of time." What are you doing today that is making a difference eternally? What is your church doing in your community that is changing lives today? Are you focused

on tomorrow or today? Is your church focused on the present or overly consumed with looking down the road?

5. God's power is immense, yet we can witness it on a personal level in our lives on a daily basis. Are you plugged into the power that God has for your life? Are you taking full advantage of that power?

FAITH CHALLENGE

1. Read some of the Scriptures in the Bible that mention God's power (e.g., Job 36:22; Pss. 68:34; 145:5; Isa. 40:10; Zech. 4:6; Acts 1:8; Rom. 1:16; 1 Cor. 1:18; Col. 1:11; Rev. 19:1). Recognize some of the areas in your life in which you are not taking advantage of God's power. Come up with an action plan for those areas and begin the necessary work to improve for the glory of God.

2. Observe five people in your church in whom you believe God's power is evident. Study their language, their attitude, their integrity and their other characteristics, and then compare their lives with yours. What common characteristics do you and those individuals share?

Session Six: God Is All-Knowing and All-Present

CHAPTERS TO READ: 5, 15, 21, 25, 28, 29, 39, 40

God is not only all-powerful, but He is also all-knowing and all-present. He knows all things past, present and future. His foreknowledge is one of His most fascinating aspects. His knowledge of all things gives us comfort for our past, present and future.

1. Nothing comes as a surprise to God. If it did, it would take away from His power. How would you define God's knowledge of the past, present and future? Do you believe that God already knows about tomorrow? How does God's knowledge of all things affect your day-to-day living?

2. God sees all and is everywhere; therefore, He knows all. In chapter 15, the authors state that "God knows all things because He is omnipresent, that means God is equally present everywhere all the time. Since He is everywhere, He knows everything that's happening." How have you felt God's presence in your life? Does the fact that God is everywhere and sees everything change the way you live your life? Does your church experience God's presence in your worship services? If so, what are the results of God's evident presence in your church?

3. Because of God's knowledge, He knows the appropriate time for all things. In chapter 21, the authors write, "God has purpose when He is waiting. He waits for people to repent of sin and turn to Him." At times, it can also seem as if God is silent (see chapter 5). What are some times in your life in which you felt God was silent? Has God ever waited to answer your prayers? Has God ever had to wait on you to follow His will in an area of your life?

4. The fact that God smiles on us when we are following His desires is an awesome picture of how great He truly is. In chapter 25, Dr. Towns notes that "when God smiles, I know He is happy with me." God is always present and always knows if we are doing what He wants. Have you experienced God's smile on your life recently? If so, why did God smile? God also frowns (see chapter 28) and is broken-hearted when individuals fail to believe in Him (see chapter 29). Is your life causing

God to smile or to frown? What about your church? Is it causing God to smile or to frown?

5. God's presence and knowledge should have high priority in
   your life and in the life of your church. Does the fact that God
   watches what you do all the time have an impact on what you
   do? Does the fact that God knows whether or not you choose
   sin over Him lead you to actually choose Him over sin? Does
   God's presence make you desire to be more like Him? What
   about your church? Do you see an awareness of God's presence
   and knowledge at work in your congregation?

FAITH CHALLENGE

1. Change your time schedule for one week and make an effort
   to spend more time alone in the presence of God. As you do,
   you will experience a deeper appreciation for His knowledge
   and presence in your life.

2. Identify those things in your life that you know God would
   not want to include in His presence. Seek out an accountabil-
   ity partner who will hold your feet to the fire on these issues.
   This will benefit you and will allow you to experience God's
   presence in your life at a greater level.

Session Seven: God Never Changes

CHAPTERS TO READ: 19, 33, 41, 42

One of the most comforting characteristics of God is that He has
not, does not, and will not ever change! God cannot improve

upon Himself; therefore, He is who He is for all of eternity. This should be a great relief to believers who live in a constantly changing world. God is our foundation of stability.

1. God never changes, but He does get weary. As the authors note in chapter 19, "God doesn't get physically tired or exhausted, but God can get weary dealing with our sins." Just because God never changes doesn't mean that we should not be changing! What are some things in your life that are "wearying" God that need to change? What are some things that don't need to change?

2. The message of the cross can never change. However, does this mean that our churches should never change? Are you in a church where you sense that your method of reaching people should be changed? If so, what would you do differently? What happens to churches that make such changes? What happens to churches that reject change?

3. If we are going to look more like Jesus, in what areas should we change our public persona? Should we look more like the world? Should we look less like the world? Why or why not?

4. Because God has no tomorrows (see chapter 33) and does not change, does this mean that He is still doing what He did in the Bible? Do you still see Him move like He did in the past? If so, where and when have you seen Him move? If not, why do you think that God doesn't move in such power or use those same methods any longer?

5. God is *Spirit*—He is immaterial, invisible and unchanging (see chapter 41). Does the fact that God is Spirit and does not change bring you comfort? Should you place your faith

in the fact that He is not going to move? Does God not changing alter the way you look at Him? Does it change the way you look at the culture? Does it change the way you read the Bible?

FAITH CHALLENGE

1. List some of the events in your life in which you were able to place your faith in an immovable God. Now go back and write a paragraph about what God taught you during those experiences.

2. Write out some of the ways that your church could change its method of reaching the lost without changing its message. List 10 ways in which your church could be more relevant in this culture without compromising the unchanging God and His message.

Session Eight: God Is Three in One

CHAPTER TO READ: 43

The doctrine of the Trinity is one of the unique aspects of the Christian faith. The fact that God the Father, Jesus the Son and the Holy Spirit the Helper are all three unique in their roles, yet the same in their nature, is awesome and mind-boggling. All three are living and active in our lives today.

1. How do you explain the Trinity to those who inquire? Do you believe that the Three are One? Does your church embrace the doctrine of the Trinity?

2. God's ability to be Spirit is in fact essential to His sovereignty. As the authors state in chapter 41, "To understand God as spirit is also to realize He can be omnipresent, or present everywhere at the same time." Do you feel God's presence through His Spirit? Do you know that His Spirit is with you all the time? Does this make you want to glorify Him with your life?

3. When you pray, do you pray to the Father, the Son and the Spirit? If not, why not? Do you believe that God the Father is equal to Jesus the Son and the Holy Spirit?

4. Although all three persons of the Trinity are active in your life, how does the Spirit relate to you on a day-to-day basis? How does Jesus affect your daily life? What does God do for you each day?

5. When you worship, do you worship all three members of the Trinity? Does this affect how you worship? Does it change your song selection in your worship service?

FAITH CHALLENGE

1. Reflect on the list of the attributes of the Trinity and the work of the Trinity in chapter 43. Make a list of all the ways that you see the Trinity at work in your life. Categorize these events by the Father, the Son and the Holy Spirit. Meditate on the ways each of these persons of the Trinity have made you look more like Jesus.

2. Write out a list of all the sins for which the Spirit is convicting you. Take time to thank God for sending His Son to die for you so that you may lay down all of these sins before Him. Repent and turn from those sins with the help of the Trinity.

ALSO BY
ELMER TOWNS

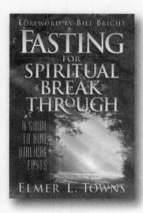

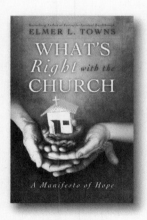